Whitman and Tradition

Daguerreotype of Walt Whitman, ca. 1854, by an unknown photographer, probably Gabriel Harrison. Courtesy of the Collection of Rare Books, William R. Perkins Library, Duke University.

Whitman and Tradition

The Poet in His Century

Kenneth M. Price

YALE UNIVERSITY PRESS

NEW HAVEN AND LONDON

Set in Palatino type by The Composing Room of
Michigan, Inc. Printed in the United States of
America by Vail-Ballou Press, Binghamton, New
York.

Library of Congress Cataloging-in-Publication Data

Price, Kenneth M.
Whitman and tradition : the poet in his
century / Kenneth M. Price
    p.   cm.
    Includes bibliographical references (p.).
    ISBN 0–300–04683–9 (alk. paper)
    1. Whitman, Walt, 1819–1892—Knowledge—
Literature.   2. Whitman, Walt, 1819–1892—
Influence.   3. Influence (Literary, artistic, etc.)
I. Title.
PS3242.L5P7   1990
811'.3—dc20   89–27380
                         CIP

The paper in this book meets the guidelines for
permanence and durability of the Committee on
Production Guidelines for Book Longevity of the
Council on Library Resources.

10 9 8 7 6 5 4 3 2 1

For Renée

 CONTENTS

 A C K N O W L E D G M E N T S

It is a pleasure to thank the many people who have helped with this book. My greatest intellectual debt is to Robert A. Ferguson: his guidance, insights, and example shaped this project from first to last. Without him, this book would not exist. C. Carroll Hollis, Robert C. Leitz III, and Vivian R. Pollak read the entire manuscript and improved it with their numerous helpful suggestions. Daniel Aaron, Roger Asselineau, Walter Blair, John W. Crowley, Edwin Haviland Miller, James E. Miller, Jr., and Marsden Price all read sections of this book, and all have had an impact on its final form. My work has also benefited from the careful editing of Ellen Graham and Caroline Murphy of Yale University Press. The editors of *Texas Studies in Literature and Language*, *ESQ: A Journal of the American Renaissance*, and *The Mickle Street Review* provided encouragement by publishing sections of chapters 1, 4, and 5. One paragraph from chapter 2, in addition, is drawn from a note published earlier in *American Literature*. I am grateful for permission to reprint these now revised sections.

A number of my colleagues at Texas A&M University have advanced this undertaking. Jerome Loving and Larry J. Reynolds commented perceptively on several chapters. Thanks also go to Dennis Berthold, William Bedford Clark, Jeffrey N. Cox, Lawrence J. Oliver, and Harrison T. Meserole for giving generously of their time and knowledge. I am indebted to two department heads—David H. Stewart and Hamlin L. Hill—and two deans—Keith Bryant and Daniel Fallon—for supporting my research. Three kind graduate students, Chryseis O. Fox, Deborah Moy, and Wu Yiqiang, helped me solve computer problems and locate materials. In addition, the Interdisciplinary Group for Historical Literary Study at Texas A&M provided a stimulating forum for the exchange of ideas.

My wife, Renée Price, has been the first judge of every chapter, and for her advice, contributions, and love I am most grateful.

 ABBREVIATIONS

The following abbreviations are used parenthetically in the text.

C   *Walt Whitman: The Correspondence*, ed. Edwin Haviland Miller, 6 vols. (New York University Press, 1961–1977).

CRE   *Walt Whitman: Leaves of Grass, Comprehensive Reader's Edition*, ed. Harold W. Blodgett and Sculley Bradley (New York: New York University Press, 1965).

LG 1855 *Leaves of Grass: The First (1855) Edition*, ed. Malcolm Cowley (New York: Viking, 1959).

LG 1856 *Leaves of Grass, Facsimile of 1856 Edition: By Walt Whitman*, intro. Gay Wilson Allen (n.p.: Norwood, 1976).

LG 1860 *Leaves of Grass, by Walt Whitman: Facsimile Edition of the 1860 Text*, intro. Roy Harvey Pearce (Ithaca, N.Y.: Cornell University Press, 1961).

NUPM *Walt Whitman: Notebooks and Unpublished Prose Manuscripts*, ed. Edward F. Grier, 6 vols. (New York: New York University Press, 1984).

xi

PW   *Walt Whitman: Prose Works, 1892,* ed. Floyd Stovall, 2 vols.
         (New York: New York University Press, 1963–1964).

WWWC   *With Walt Whitman in Camden,* ed. Horace Traubel, 6 vols.
         (vol. 1, Boston: Small, Maynard & Co., 1906; 2–3, New
         York: Mitchell Kennerley, 1915; 4, Philadelphia: University
         of Pennsylvania Press, 1953; 5–6, Carbondale: University
         of Southern Illinois Press, 1964, 1982).

 PROLOGUE

This study looks backward and forward from that moment in the nineteenth century when Walt Whitman sauntered into literature. My primary concern is with Whitman's negotiations with his literary pasts (and thereby with the nature of his creativity) and with the negotiations his first followers held with him. For writers, tradition is inevitably a literary transaction but is never that alone; tradition also bears on the way writers accept and alter literature's place in the world.[1] Hence, I focus on literary works while keeping a broader social field in view. Too often influence studies give the impression that authors live in an isolated and timeless realm made up of literary immortals. Such studies can ignore the importance of book reviews and other minor writing, the power of publishers and censors, the role of immediate audiences of all kinds, and the significance of the academy. Yet if we ignore how literature functions within the world, we cannot hope to understand how ideas, works, and reputations actually survive in transmission or how reputations rise and fall, sometimes to rise again.

For comprehensible professional and historical reasons, critics have often regarded American literature as an exclusive domain. Because of the "literary nationalist tendency," that habit of isolating what are thought to be authentically American traits in a work for discussion and praise, we fail to perceive strengths in such writers as Longfellow, and we fail to see that many of the "native" qualities of Whitman resulted from his opposition to foreign influence.[2] Writers of the last century typically experienced not isolated national traditions but a complex Anglo-American culture. The common use of the English language united Englishmen and Americans in profound and (particularly for Americans) sometimes painful ways. Robert Weisbuch has argued persuasively that writers of the American Renaissance started out from "a defensive position and . . . the achievements of British literature and British national life [were] the chief intimidations" against which they, as American representatives, defended themselves.[3] American writers were shaped by snide British pronouncements about the incompatibility of democracy and art.

One key American defense against these remarks was to manipulate the cultural clock. The culture the British promoted as rich and mature became less threatening and inhibiting when Americans conceived of it as old and jaded, a culture on the wane. Thus Whitman recurrently claimed that "ennui" characterized British life and art. Americans were not uniformly critical, however: they willingly attributed greater value and vigor to earlier periods of English literature. Americans could allude to Chaucer, Spenser, Shakespeare, and Milton in an untroubled, often reverential manner by regarding them as part of a common inheritance. This half-truth allowed American writers to draw on early British literature without the competitiveness displayed by, say, Blake and Shelley when confronting Milton. With the English romantics the Americans engaged in a struggle similar to the one the English romantics themselves held with Milton. But it was with their exact contemporaries, the Victorians, that the real wrangling began; it was the Victorians, after all, who were their competitors for shelf space in bookstores and for public approbation. Like other Americans, Whitman argues most forcefully with his near predecessors and contemporaries. Yet in his assertive early phase, Whitman stands alone in his sweeping rejection of English greats, including Milton and Shakespeare, a rejection perhaps necessary for his own claim to greatness and for the establishment of a distinctive poetic voice.

In his manipulations of cultural time, Whitman frequently placed himself at a mythic beginning, oriented toward the future. His tradition building, then, demonstrates the falsity of the widely held assumption that the tradition monger is inevitably conservative and regressive. Whether a tradition is conservative depends on circumstances and on the nature of the antagonist.[4] In 1855, when Whitman seized the oppositional role, he could still depict the current practice of English and American poetry as a monolithic target, a single orthodoxy. English *and* American poets, he argued, were writing English poetry inappropriate to a modern, democratic age.

American-centered criticism has produced two familiar approaches to Whitman studies: first, depictions of the poet as a primitive genius, an American Adam, who achieved "originality" by reaching back to a primal era or by operating apart from literary tradition, and second, depictions of him as *the* Emersonian poet. These views need to be qualified and given greater complexity. Although there has been much discussion of Whitman the "rough" (just as the poet wanted), I explore here his connections with literary culture. Whitman actively discouraged such an approach: "it is not on 'Leaves of Grass' distinctively as *literature*, or a specimen thereof, that I feel to dwell, or advance claims. No one will get at my verses who insists upon viewing them as a literary performance, or attempt at such performance" (*CRE*, p. 574). But there is good reason to ask disqualified questions. A pressing need to establish one's legitimacy implies a threat to it. The mythical past Whitman created operated as a defensive strategy in a real present.[5] The sheer energy of Whitman's denials of connectedness with literary high culture, particularly in his great early phase, suggests that more attention should be paid to his defensive strategy. Only by placing the poet in the literary context he so often tried to expunge can we comprehend the nature of his adversarial role.

In the following chapters I examine key episodes of literary interaction to clarify how Whitman and literary tradition functioned within particular cultural settings. Each chapter provides a case study that leads to a more inclusive overview. My immediate goals are, first, to increase understanding of the norms within which Whitman worked and from which he deviated and, second, to reformulate the legacy he left. A larger goal is to contribute to the discussion of tradition itself through the example of Whitman. I have not confined myself to studying Whitman and a single tradition because, like other writers, the poet experienced a wealth of competing, changing, and interpenetrating traditions. Of course, to determine which past a writer draws on—out of the many possible pasts—is a crucial interpretive act.

The first tradition Whitman invented, already mentioned, was an oxymoronic tradition without a past—rather, with a radically foreshortened past—a tradition in which Whitman himself became the past as he wrote and thus became the significant heritage for writers he imagined, the "poets to come." He could assert this myth only through a massive denial of major nineteenth-century English poets. My study begins by reconstructing, on the basis of Whitman's private documents, the unacknowledged, suppressed, but nonetheless operative English heritage. Of particular interest is the way Whitman is tied, through negation, to the romantics and Tennyson. In 1856 Whitman advanced an alternative version of poetic lineage when he installed Emerson as "master" and himself and others as followers. Yet Whitman's depiction of himself as a follower is closer to his pose as the initiating figure than has been realized because he undermines his created "master." When we move to an examination of individual poems, we can see that the significant past for Whitman was more complicated than is suggested by either of his early poses, the poet as primal originator or the poet as Emersonian disciple. Further, we can perceive that what was meaningful and useful changed over the four decades of his writing career. We can also understand the importance of reconstructing *his* sense of the past. We must, for example, reconceive of Longfellow and Bryant as giants, so that we properly recollect Whitman's tenuous place in the literary world, so that we reevaluate Whitman's search for an audience in light of what seemed possible in his time.

My closing chapters explore how the poet first became a usable past for later writers. Paradoxically, the attempt by the Boston attorney general to ban Whitman from the mail in order to lessen his impact in the present of 1881 made him an especially meaningful past for writers at the close of the century. Whereas Hawthorne's place in tradition was first firmly established because of the canon-making power of James T. Fields's publishing ventures, Whitman's place was ensured by attempts at exclusion that backfired. Those Gilded Age writers who linked themselves with Hawthorne reached for a particular kind of cultural authority, for he was a legitimated, institutionally sanctioned literary figure as early as the 1850s. Those who aligned themselves with Whitman often did so as an act of protest and typically asserted the importance of the role (real or imagined) of outsider.

Not surprisingly, the poets who first drew on Whitman were dissatisfied with prevailing poetic and social norms. The Harvard poets—particularly George Cabot Lodge and William Vaughn Moody—were uncomfortable as Cambridge insiders in an age when New England domination of American high culture reached its peak. Whitman has been a "courage-giver" to many great poets in the twentieth century, but, as Richard Brodhead points out, he "became the great enabler he is (for instance) for Hart Crane's or William Carlos Williams's poetic assertions only after a change in . . . institutions brought him to the center of our poetic history: made him a past poets could possess and work out of."[6] Questions remain: Why and how was Whitman brought "to the center"? And who in key institutions brought change about? My final chapter explores this juncture between the refusal to admit Whitman into the organized past and the conversion of him into a "great enabler," a juncture little understood because of the critical habit of tracing influence through "strong" poets and disregarding minor ones.

The importance of studying Whitman and tradition is suggested by Roy Harvey Pearce's remark that American poetry of the twentieth century is "in essence if not in substance, a series of arguments with Whitman. . . . If [poets] battled against Whitman and Whitmanism, the battle—whether or not they could bring themselves to admit it—was on his terms and on his grounds." His impact on the novel, far less adequately studied, has also been profound: an extraordinary array of writers, including Dreiser, Wharton, Dos Passos, Wolfe, Kerouac, Bellow, Jim Harrison, and others, have drawn on Whitman. In a passing comment, Harold Bloom has described him as an "inescapable influence" on writers of American fiction.[7] The figurative language employed by Pearce and Bloom carries the implication that authors ordinarily fight or flee a great predecessor. Certainly the idea that a literary precursor is threatening has become, in the past few decades, the dominant way to consider literary influence. But the ways in which the past impinges on the present are infinitely varied, and we need to avoid artificially limiting—because of our metaphors or zeitgeist—what the past can do. Much is gained by being equally ready to find the past enabling, sustaining, funding, and empowering as it is impoverishing, inhibiting, and debilitating.

Emerson and Hawthorne have been fountainheads of tradition equal to Whitman in an isolated American context. No other American writer, however, can match Whitman's impact on world literature. From Ivan Turgenev to Pablo Neruda, from D. H. Lawrence to Thomas Mann, from Guo Moruo to Fernando Pessoa, Whitman's influence radiates outward in all directions. I am most interested in the source and center of the radiations, and thus I study the poet in his century and in Anglo-American culture, where the radiations began.

CHAPTER ONE

"An American bard at last!" Whitman's Persona and the English Heritage

*I*n 1856 Henry David Thoreau speculated about the character of America's newest poet. "Since I have seen him," he wrote of Walt Whitman, "I find that I am not disturbed by any brag or egoism in his book. He may turn out the least of a braggart of all, having a better right to be confident."[1] With the first two editions of *Leaves of Grass* behind him (1855, 1856) and with Emerson's famous letter of praise fresh in mind, Whitman had some reason for self-assurance. Yet Whitman's assertiveness preceded his great literature. In the 1840s and early 1850s, when his creative output consisted of nothing more than some good journalism, undistinguished fiction, and derivative poetry, Whitman was already describing himself as a great bard and audaciously criticizing some of the most notable English poets.

This early assertiveness toward the English is related to what was perhaps Whitman's most crucial breakthrough, the creation of a recognizable and distinct persona. A key to understanding the persona is Whitman's aspiration: he consistently imagined not the poet but the "great poet," the "true poet," the "divine bard," the "divine literatus." With few obvious credentials other than the power of his will, he made himself into "a master after my own kind."[2]

The development of Walt out of Walter was such a liberating, enabling, and empowering experience that he never tired of describing either the act or the result, his created self. Paul Zweig once observed that perhaps no other poet ever wrote so many third-person self-portraits.[3] The evidence suggests that Whitman's self-assertions were rooted in fear: a person ill at ease with his sexuality became the virile bard, a failed politician sensitive to social fragmentation elevated America to the "greatest poem," the product of a family riddled with disease and neuroses celebrated the poet of "perfect health." Thus it is not surprising that we find in "albot Wilson" (the notebook begun in 1847 and containing the first musings of the developing poet) a concern with Old World standards and assertions of mastery intermixed with fears of dependence:

> True noble expanding American character is raised on a far more lasting and universal basis than that of any of the characters of the "gentlemen" of aristocratic life, or of novels, or under the European or Asian forms of society or government.—It is to be illimitably proud, independent, self-possessed generous and gentle. . . . It is to be poor, rather than rich—but to prefer death sooner than any mean dependence.—Prudence is part of it, because prudence is the right arm of independence.

> Every American young man should carry himself with the finished and haughty bearing of the greatest ruler and proprietor—for he is a great ruler and proprietor—the greatest.

> Great latitude must be allowed to others

Play your muscle, and it will be lithe as caoutchouc and strong as iron—I wish to see American young men the workingmen, carry themselves with a high horse/

Where is the being of which I am the inferior?—It is the [word missing] of the sly or shallow to divide men like the metals into those more precious and others less precious, intrinsically

I never yet knew how it felt to think I stood in the presence of my superior.—*If the presence of* God were made visible immediately before me, I could not abase myself.—How do I know but I shall myself

I will not be the cart, nor the load on the cart, nor the horses that draw the cart; but I will be the little hands that guide the cart. [*NUPM* 1:56]

Whitman's swings from extreme to extreme are revealing: he claims that he looks, apparently in vain, for "the being of which I am the inferior," only to outdo that by noting that he could not abase himself even to God. Yet he also worries about those who "divide men like the metals into those more precious and others less precious, intrinsically." Sensitive to claims that democracy promoted mediocrity and concerned that he was approaching mid-life with few solid accomplishments behind him, Whitman begins to articulate his paradoxical vision of democratic potential. He anticipates the hopeful logic-stretching of 1855 when he asserts that "every American young man should carry himself with the finished and haughty bearing of the greatest ruler and proprietor—for he is a great ruler and proprietor—the greatest." Such a claim is in keeping with Whitman's discussions of the "divine average" and with his claim in the Preface that there can be "unnumbered Supremes" (*LG 1855*, p. 13). Consistently, Whitman struggles to reconcile a commitment to the common and average while promoting the great and heroic.

Whitman's persona was many things the man was not: lazy, rude, rough, reckless, abandoned, free of racial prejudice, and the begetter of children. But no assumed feature is more striking than Whitman's early accounts of his own greatness in the absence of justifying accomplishments. We are so accustomed to stressing the miraculous nature of Whitman's transformation, so intent on stressing the differences between Walter and Walt, that we sometimes lose sight of this transformation's context. Familial forces, for instance, were crucial in encouraging Whitman to remake himself and in providing suggestions about how to do it. He assumed a role in the family that mirrored in many ways the role he adopted as a poet.

His family situation contributed to radical swings between despair and elation. Within the nuclear unit, Whitman could sense potential greatness (in himself and in his brother Jeff), but he could also see sordid degeneration. Knowledge of the family helps illuminate curious passages, such as the following one from Whitman's notebooks:

> The effusion or corporation of the soul is always under the beautiful laws of physiology—I guess the soul can never be any ? thing but great and pure and immortal; but it makes itself visible only through matter—a perfect head, and bowels and bones to match is the easy gate through which it comes from its embowered garden, and pleasantly appears to the sight of the world.—A twisted skull, and blood watery or rotten by ancestry or gluttony, or rum or bad disorders,— they are the darkness toward which the plant will not grow, although its seed lies waiting for ages.—[*NUPM* 1:58]

With an emotionally unstable sister and with one brother syphilitic, another alcoholic, and a third physically and mentally retarded, Whitman witnessed many "bad disorders." Remarkably, out of this milieu, Walt stressed the heartiness of the Whitman line and the glory of his own perfect health.

Whitman's claims to be the divine bard, the central man, the culture-healer, and the seedsman are, then, the reverse side of terrifying concerns. He felt marginalized by troubling doubts about his sexual orientation, by his artisan-class status, by his relative failures professionally, by his childless future.[4] Frequently at odds with his namesake father, he saw in Walter Whitman, Sr., an example of economic decline and personality disorder. His mother, however, provided crucial support. She helped her son define a place for himself in the family that also illuminates his poetic role.

Louisa Van Velsor Whitman saw Walt as her special child. On a visit to Brooklyn, Bronson Alcott and Henry Thoreau learned from the poet's mother that Walt had always been for the "weaker against the stronger, and the umpire in all disputes." She made it clear that, though she knew Walt had his faults, she thought him "an extraordinary son of a fond mother."[5] By 1847, at age twenty-eight—the most likely time for his first experimental poetry—he was buying boots for his brothers and held the title to the family home, even though his father was to live another eight years. Increasingly Louisa came to depend on Walt, until in the mid-1860s he had become, in her words, the "old standby," her "sole reliance," her "whole dependence."[6] Walt learned to be the provider and adjudicator in the family—roles he attributed to the ideal poet.

Whitman's family background also contributed to his paradoxical view of democracy. He often used the figure of the mother as an emblem for American democracy; that he was thinking in particular of his own mother Louisa is suggested by the following passage: "For this circling Confederacy, standing together with interlinked hands, ample, equal, each one with his grip of love wedged in life or in death to all the rest, we must share and share alike. Our old mother does not spread the table with a fine dish for one and scraps for another.—She teaches us no such mean and hoggish lesson.—If there be any of good dish and not enough of it to go completely round, it shall not be brought on at all" (*NUPM* 6:2178–79). Yet if all the children were treated equally in the Whitman family, Louisa also left Walt assured that he was her favorite. She told him once, "Write on a paper loose from the letter if you say anything you dont want all to read." She confided in Walt about family frustrations, so much so that in at least three cases she instructed him to "burn this letter." He, too, would sometimes write for her eyes only, for she reported burning one of his letters. When a crucial decision was pending for Walt's brother George, she turned to Walt for advice: "write just what you think would be best . . . walt write it just to me and not for the family." Her final words in her deathbed letter reveal her primary loyalty: "farewell my beloved sons farewell i have lived byond all comfort in the world dont mourn for me my beloved sons and daughters farewell my dear beloved walter."[7] In the family Walt was ostensibly an equal but actually above while still alongside. The paradox of this situation lives on in the complex role of the poet who, though like the common people, possesses the vision they lack.

The Margin of Confidence: Young Walt
Whitman on English Poets and Poetry

Whitman's fears—political, cultural, genealogical, sexual— were real, but he controlled most of them in the years preceding *Leaves of Grass*. The poet's growing confidence is nowhere more apparent than in his response to English poetry. Whereas other American poets deferred to the English tradition, Whitman challenged virtually all his "foreign" predecessors. In the long "foreground" of *Leaves of Grass*, Whitman annotated magazine and book clippings, many of which dealt with English poets and poetics.[8] These annotations deserve careful attention, for they reveal much about the nature of Whitman's creative drive, about his goals for poetry, and about the shaping of his ideas.[9] In his private quarrels with other poets—for so his annotations appear—Whitman relied on a firm sense of self and country to qualify and circumscribe the major intellectual influences on his work. One may go farther. Whitman's poetics probably took shape in the heat of this exchange.

The importance of Whitman's attitude toward the English heritage can best be understood if we place his comments in a broad American context. Despite many calls for a national literature in the nineteenth century, American poets themselves had expressed profound doubts about the suitability of America for poetry. William Cullen Bryant's qualification of negations was hardly reassuring: the scientific bent of Americans, he argued, does not make them fundamentally antipoetic. James Russell Lowell was more forthright about some terrible fears: "It may not be our destiny to produce a great literature."[10] Even poets who were more optimistic about America's literary future often expressed their hopes in terms that seemed obsessed with limitation. Oliver Wendell Holmes, John Greenleaf Whittier, and Ralph Waldo Emerson successively argued that the lack of strength and boldness in American poets "is not a necessary consequence of their country or education." After all, Whittier remarked, "the proud blood of England's mightiest courses through their veins."[11] These and similar assertions actually underscore American doubts. Whitman, in contrast, claimed that "the Americans of all nations at any time upon the earth have probably the fullest poetical nature. The United States themselves are essentially the greatest poem." Others might reassure themselves with thoughts of their English blood; Whitman scorned the very idea. The poetry of England, "that wonderful *little* island," grows out of the "facts of the English race, the monarchy and aristocracy prominent over the rest" (italics added). Such a literature is unacceptable for a land of democratic politics and ample geography like America: "No nation ever did or ever will receive with national affection any poets except those born of its national blood."[12]

The general insecurity of American poets appears again and again in their insistence that Shakespeare belonged as much to Americans as to the English. Lowell adopted a tone of incredulity toward those who assumed otherwise: "As if Shakespeare, sprung from the race and the class which colonized New England, had not been also ours!" Milton, too, could be a part of American literature, thus covering the nakedness that many felt in the absence of an indigenous poetic tradition.[13] But whereas others tried to graft the English tradition onto the American psyche, Whitman called instead for writers "essentially different from the old poets, and from the modern successions of jinglers and snivellers and fops." Even Shakespeare needed to be rejected: "In the verse of all those undoubtedly great writers, Shakspere just as much as the rest, there is the air which to America is the air of death."[14]

Whittier, Emerson, and Edgar Allan Poe occasionally attacked individual English poets, but even the sharpest of their criticisms recognized a controlling influence.[15] All agreed with Poe's judicious statement: "In paying [the English], as a nation, a respectful and not undue deference to a supremacy rarely questioned but by prejudice or ignorance, we should, of course, be doing nothing more than acting in a rational manner. The *excess* of our subserviency was blameable."[16] No American before Whitman dared fault the influence of Shakespeare and Milton. He alone challenged the supremacy of the tradition as a whole.

Despite Whitman's iconoclastic ways—or perhaps because of them—the poet learned much from the English tradition. Yet as the poet gained knowledge, he bent it to his purposes. One review Whitman annotated discussed how a creative mind might profit from ordinary ideas: "It is the privilege of genius . . . to extract their gold dust out of the most worthless books."[17] When a highbrow reviewer suggested one should read only difficult writers, Whitman argued with him in the margin: "Still all kinds of light reading, novels, newspapers, gossip etc, serve as manure for the few *great productions,* and are indispensable or perhaps are premises to something better" (see figure 1).[18] This observation is telling, for it accurately describes Whitman's ability to use what he does not necessarily accept. The metaphor of conventional thought as indispensable manure implies a proper balance between disrespect and use, a kind of transmutation of predecessors that lends itself to the creation of a distinctive theory.

Two suggestive remarks from 1855 help explain Whitman's remarkable ability to use influences while keeping them within limits. One way in which the poet limited English influence was to stress his American identity: "What very properly fits a subject of the British crown may fit very ill an American freeman."[19] Whitman revised all suggestions provided by English poets, remolding ideas to conform with his democratic outlook. But Whitman's democratic outlook is paradoxical: the poet is the heroic commoner, one of the "divine average." Whitman managed to make the tensions inherent in this conception a source of strength. Note, for example, how Whitman used paradox and balance as a second way to protect himself from influence. He never allowed "sympathy" to overwhelm his "pride": "The soul has that measureless pride which consists in never acknowledging any lessons but its own. But it has sympathy as measureless as its pride and

Figure 1. Whitman's marginalia. Courtesy of the Collection of Rare Books, William R. Perkins Library, Duke University.

deed, he has; but he has no idea of writing such a thing as *you* call a book. He wrote to make you wiser, not to make you lazier, or himself richer. That he wrote to make you think, not to divert you from thinking, is the very thing that makes him worth your reading, and the only thing that makes anyone worth your reading. For it is not the idleness with which we read, but the very intensity of labor which our reading calls forth, that does us good. We are benefited not so much by the attainment, as by the earnest pursuit of truth. To *think* ourselves into error, is far better than to *sleep* ourselves into truth. If the Lord had designed we should be wise and happy without thought, he would have made us brutes, and done with it. The easy picking-up and pocketing of an author's thoughts, is good for nothing but to help us along in intellectual foppery. It is the severe labor of thinking, producing a development or expansion of the faculties, that makes the worth of reading. An author enriches us, not so much by giving us his ideas, as by unfolding in us the same powers that originated them. Reading, in short, if it be truly such, and not a mere imparted mental drowsiness, involves a development of the same activities, and a voluntary reproduction of the same states of mind, of which the author was subject in writing. The divine light reading, which is deified so much, can serve no earthly purpose, but to make us light-headed; the more we take of it, the emptier shall we assuredly become. Flour may indeed be baked and eaten without much labor, but will not grow; and seed-wheat will produce nothing without patient toil and tillage. Knowest thou not, that the bread which thou eatest without the sweat of thy brow, can be no bread to thee? Why, it will turn into poison, and kill you with the gout, or the apoplexy, or some such disease. Would exercise be good for anything unless it exercised us? Most assuredly all good reading is hard work; nay it is good chiefly *because* it is hard, plucking our laziness by the nose, in order to give us health and strength. If an author do anything but revive our old thoughts in a new dress, assuredly we must work to follow him; and if that be all he does, why not let him alone and cultivate a few sprouts of our own? That the literature in question is utterly worthless, is proven by the fact, that it keeps people constantly eating, without ever feeding them.—While their hunger and thirst of soul remain unsatisfied, they keep crying, give, give, ignorant that they are starving from a defect in the quality, not in the quantity of their food. They ask for bread and literature gives them wind; nevertheless, they down with whatever comes to them, thinking their hunger continues because they have not enough, not because they have mere wind. They may cry, peace, peace, as much as they please; but there is no peace for them, till they have some work. Such, at least, is our hope. He who truly *reads* a few genuine books, a few "books that are books," will spend much of his time in thinking; he who is too lazy to think at all, will probably spend all of his time in reading. We can digest wind much easier than bacon.

But reading without thought, bad as it is, is little if any worse than reading with too much thought, People often defeat their own efforts, by reading to give rather than get instruction. In the words of Goethe, they undertake to oversee an author, before they get to see him. Sterne very naturally wished for a reader who, yielding up the reins of his faculties into the hands of his author, would be content to be pleased, he knew not why and cared not wherefore. A compliance with this wish would no doubt be as beneficial to readers, as satisfactory to authors. For the only good reason for reading an author is, that he knows more of what he is writing about than we do. If an author be truly worth the reading, it will be long enough before we get to see him; and when we get competent to oversee him, it would really seem hardly worth our while to trouble our heads about him. All true books are but spectacles to read nature with; and all true readers employ these, to look *through*, not to look *at*. If we cannot look through them, then they are not spectacles to us, but only gewgaws; and what is the use of playing with them, and looking at them, and criticizing them? Moreover, it is not by speaking this truth or that truth, our truth or your truth, but by simply speaking truth, what is true to him, that a man shames the devil. The devil himself sometimes tells truth; but he does it hypocritically, and therefore is only the more devilish for telling it. It is an author's business to give us his thoughts and feelings, not to reflect our own; to be our teacher, not our looking-glass. The genuineness of his writings consists in their truth to Na-

Still all kinds of light reading novels newspapers gossip &c. serve as manure for the few great productions, and are indispensable or perhaps are premises to something better.— The whole raff of light reading is also a testimony in honor of the original good reading which preceded it.— The thousands of common poets, romancers, essayists and attempters, exist because some twenty or fifty geniuses at intervals led the way long before.

the one balances the other and neither can stretch too far while it stretches in company with the other. The inmost secrets of art sleep with the twain. The greatest poet has lain close betwixt both and they are vital in his style and thoughts" (*LG 1855*, p. 12). Whitman's poetic sympathy allowed him to benefit from others and to make his learning "vital"; his pride moved him beyond a merely arrogant denial of others' achievements to an assertion of the radical importance of the poet's personal identity. We can better understand Whitman's statement about pride and sympathy by noting his reaction to Keats's definition of poetic identity, which he read in an anonymous review of R. M. Milnes's *Life, Letters, and Literary Remains of John Keats:*

> As to the poetical character itself (I mean that sort of which, if I am anything, I am a member, that sort distinguished from the Wordsworthian, or egotistical sublime, which is a thing *per se*, and stands alone), it is not itself—it has no self—it is everything and nothing. It has no character. . . . It has as much delight in conceiving an Iago as an Imogene. What shocks the virtuous philosopher delights the c[h]ameleon poet. . . . A poet is the most unpoetical of anything in existence, because he has no identity; he is continually in for and filling some other body. . . . When I am in a room with people, if I am free from speculating on creations of my own brain, then, not myself goes home to myself; but the identity of every one in the room begins to press upon me, so that I am in a very little time annihilated.

Whitman responded in the margin: "The great poet absorbs the Iden[ti]ty and the expe[rience] of others, and they are definite in him or from him; but he p[resses] them all through the powerful press of himself . . . his own masterly identity."[20] Like Keats, Whitman thinks the poet should so fully sympathize with others that their identities mesh, but unlike Keats, he insists that the poet must nonetheless retain a firm sense of personal self. For Whitman, the poet's own character was always of utmost importance: "Understand that you can have in your writing no qualities which you do not honestly entertain in yourself.—Understand that you cannot keep out of your writing the indication of the evil or shallowness you entertain in yourself. . . . There is no trick or cunning, no art or recipe, by which you can have in your writing that which you do not possess in yourself."[21] This passage may suggest that the issue of sincerity, along with that of identity, informed Whitman's reaction to Keats's letter.

Whitman's statement about the "powerful press of himself" clarifies his differences with other nineteenth-century theorists over the role of the poet's own bodily senses in the act of contemplation. Wordsworth describes the poetic moment as that "serene and blessed mood" when "we are laid asleep / In body, and become a living soul." Coleridge argues that genius in the fine arts "must act on the feeling, that body is but a striving to become mind,—that it is mind in its essence!"[22] Whitman agrees with his English counterparts on the importance of "high exalted musing," but he differs in maintaining that active senses are always involved in the highest contemplation: "a trance, yet with all the senses alert—only a state of high exalted musing—the tangible and material with all its shows, the objective world suspended or surmounted for a while, & the powers in exaltation, freedom, vision—yet the *senses* not lost or counteracted."[23] Whitman believed that by retaining bodily awareness even when ordinary thought was suspended, he could create something more compelling than what currently prevailed: namely, "non-personality and indistinctness" in modern poetry (*CRE*, p. 737).

The ability to absorb the experiences of others is, of course, linked to a poet's capacity for sympathy. Recognizing the importance of this quality to the poet, Whitman underscored a sentence in an essay on "Modern Poetry and Poets" that declared, "Sympathy is, in truth, but versatility of heart; and large sympathies are, therefore, the most powerful auxiliaries of poetic genius."[24]

Whitman was convinced that poets should show sympathy with common men and women by presenting them with dignity in literature. He agreed with a reviewer who, critical of Shelley's ethereal flights, argued that "the sphere of the true poet is among the common elements of humanity." Whitman marked similar passages criticizing both Tennyson and Wordsworth for maintaining a false sense of superiority.[25] Joining the attack, he declared in a marginal comment that "Wordsworth lacks sympathy with men and women—that does not pervade him enough by a long shot."[26] Lack of real feeling for common humanity was, he believed, the general political failing of English poets: "Of the leading British poets many who began with the rights of man abjured their beginning and came out for kingcraft priestcraft, obedience and so forth.—Southey, Coleridge, and Wordsworth did so."[27]

Whitman objected to many descriptive passages in romantic poetry because these, too, seemed manifestations of an insufficient regard for common man.[28] He marked passages in two reviews arguing that the poets of antiquity regarded "picturesque nature as so entirely subordinate to man, that they have hardly left us a single poetical landscape."[29] Both the reviewers in question felt that landscape was a mere accessory for the ancients, whose main interest was in the human or superhuman beings inhabiting the world. These notions may have suggested or confirmed Whitman's resolution of 1855: the work of the American poet is to be "indirect and not direct or descriptive" (*LG 1855*, p. 8).

Whereas a poet like Wordsworth was open to criticism because of his descriptive passages, a poet like Coleridge was vulnerable because of his reliance on the supernatural and mythical.

Several of Whitman's ideas about sanity, modernity, and the importance of common humanity contribute to a comment written in the margin of "Taylor's Eve of the Conquest": "The perfect poem is simple, healthy, natural—no griffins, angels, centaurs—no hysterics or blue fire—no dyspepsia, no suicidal intentions."[30] Romanticism generally had encouraged a revitalization of myth,[31] but Whitman objected to it as inappropriate to modernity. His dislike of myth (the early Whitman never acknowledged that his own program was powerful myth-making) probably contributed to his harsh judgment of Keats's poetry: "Of life in the nineteenth century it has none any more than the statues have."[32]

On similar grounds Whitman objected to the romantic poets' polished poetic surfaces and heavy reliance on simile and metaphor. With evident approval he marked a passage in a review criticizing Shelley for his indulgent use of figures.[33] Moreover, he wrote "truth of style" above one column of a review of "Taylor's Eve of the Conquest" that argued, "A deficiency of truthfulness in style . . . displays itself first by a superabundance of figures."[34] Whitman felt that ornate, elaborately finished poetry failed to meet the "direct wants of the bodies and souls of the [nineteenth] century." Hence he found Keats's poetry to be "ornamental, elaborated, rich in wrought imagery . . . [and] imbued with the sentiment, at second-hand, of the gods and goddesses of twenty-five hundred years ago."[35] In reaction Whitman established the severest of goals for his own verse: *"No ornamental similes at all—not one: perfect transparent clearness* sanity and health are wanted—*that* is the *divine style."* In his early poetry, Whitman used far more metonymies and fewer metaphors than other nineteenth-century British and American poets. He turned to metonymy to attain that "transparent clearness," for the metonymist may be said to present life rather than to interpret it. Moreover, as C. Carroll Hollis has observed, "the preponderance of metonymy in the early editions presupposes a mind fascinated with and glorying in the realistic details of American life."[36] Thus, Whitman claims that his modern democratic style is "divine" even as he stresses the "sturdy" and the common.[37]

Whitman was not simply rejecting heavily metaphoric language but was trying to establish a new relationship between poetry and time. According to John F. Lynen, who has focused on Whitman's treatment of time in discussing the poet's attitude toward his literary predecessors, Whitman held that traditional forms were not only distanced from contemporary facts but were detached "from the present as it existed at any time." Hence, art becomes what Whitman called "mythical" as opposed to "demonstrable." Lynen argues that the romantic poem typically progresses, "portraying a change rather than a static duration. . . . It remained for Whitman to make the poem itself constitute a determinate present moment, so that all statements have the status of speech now being spoken, and all things perceived seem to exist as objects now appearing to consciousness. . . . Instead of an event, his subject could be an activity or continuing process, and the poem could then end, not when the action is completed, but when its meaning and significance are so fully realized that no more need be said."[38] It is possible that Whitman first encountered the idea of a verse of the present in a discussion of *Paradise Lost* in "Christopher under Canvass." One of the speakers in this essay argues that the Seventh Book could not have been written in prose because "without Verse it could not have been read! The Verse makes present. You listen with Adam and Eve, and you hear the Archangel. In Prose this illusion could not have been carried through such subject-matter." Whitman both underlined "The Verse makes present" and wrote the sentence out for himself in the top margin.[39] This germ of an idea may have developed into the poet's pervasive desire to achieve temporal immediacy.[40]

Whitman refused to follow those English theorists who implied that the present lacked the grandeur of the past. In the review of "Taylor's Eve of the Conquest," Whitman marked a discussion of the modern character with underscorings, wavy lines in the margin, and three pointing hands. This reviewer argued that "aids and appliances," the "shield of law," social uniformity, the division of labor, industrialism, and the moral and intellectual cross-currents inevitable in a period of diffused knowledge all tended to limit individual robustness and make the great character rarer than in simpler times. Whitman's hopes for democracy and for himself as a poet made it impossible for him to accept this conclusion. "I will take all these things that produce this condition," he wrote, "and make them produce as great characters as any."[41] In the notebook passage cited above concerning "True noble expanding American character" Whitman explained how this might be done.

To Whitman's way of thinking, many English poets lacked "proud, independent" character because of debasing financial dealings. An article on the "Prelude" that discussed Wordsworth's dependence on patronage provoked this comment: "So it seems Wordsworth made 'a good thing' from the start, out of his poetry. legacies,! a fat office! pensions from the crown!" In the top margin of another article, "Recollections of Poets Laureate," Whitman wrote: "Tennyson has a pension of £200 a year, conferred by the Queen, some years since." (One comment on this did not suffice; Whitman repeated the information in the side margin.) The American poet admired neither the dependent position of his English counterparts nor their reliance on a governing aristocracy. The true poet, he said in his 1855 Preface, should "despise riches."[42]

Even more crucial than financial independence to both poets and individuals was the proper balancing of faith and intellect.

Like at least one of the reviewers he read, Whitman feared that the critical spirit of the age could undermine faith and hinder poetic creativity. Not surprisingly, Whitman was very interested in the following passage in the review of Milnes's *Life of Keats:* "An analytical spirit, fatal to the production, though conducive, under certain circumstances, to the enjoyment of the highest art, is the life of criticism. Criticism, in modern times, has attained to an unprecedented excellence; and this has been the result of an unprecedented development of consciousness. Into the question of the general absence of faith, which is the cause, and too often the consequence of such consciousness, we must not enter, although it is closely allied to our subject." The anonymous reviewer believed that at least some great art was produced in this age: "Wordsworth, Goethe, and Coleridge, have been the offspring of our intensely critical era."[43] Though the reviewer hesitated to discuss the connection between critical consciousness and the absence of faith, Whitman throughout his career shows a readiness to confront this issue.[44] Either by reading this article or by some other means, Whitman came to believe than an analytical consciousness—though not evil in itself—needed to be counterbalanced by more primitive forces. As he made clear in the 1855 Preface, he admired "that indescribable freshness and *unconsciousness* about an illiterate person that humbles and mocks the power of the noblest expressive genius" (*LG 1855,* p. 9; italics added). Whitman wanted to combine in himself expressive genius and what he considered to be the power and excellence of an illiterate person. He would not be the offspring of a critical era. One result was a pose so powerful that it is often not distinguished from the man: "To give judgment on real poems, one needs an account of the poet himself. . . . Politeness this man has none, and regulation he has none. A rude child of the people! . . . [He] likes the ungenteel ways of laborers . . . eats cheap fare, likes the strong flavored coffee of the coffee-stands in the market, at sunrise—likes a supper of oysters fresh from the oyster-smack—likes to make one at the crowded table among sailors and work-people—would leave a select soiree of elegant people any time to go with tumultuous men."[45]

Shortly after the appearance of the 1855 *Leaves of Grass*, Whitman published several anonymous reviews of his work, one of which was entitled "An English and an American Poet." Whitman, contradicting his own belief that the standard of nature ought to be the test of literature, compares his verse to that of Tennyson, "the best of the school of poets at present received in Great Britain and America."[46]

Whitman felt that the lack of modernity, optimism, and democratic outlook in English poetry could be traced to the cultural milieu:

> Poetry, to Tennyson and his British and American eleves, is a gentleman of the first degree, boating, fishing, and shooting genteelly through nature, admiring the ladies, and talking to them, in company, with that elaborate half-choked deference that is to be made up by the terrible license of men among themselves. . . . He meets the nobility and gentry halfway. . . . Both have the same supercilious elegance, both love the reminiscences which extol caste . . . both hold the same undertone of church and state, both have the same languishing melancholy and irony . . . both devour themselves in solitary lassitude. . . . The present phases of high-life in Great Britain are as natural a growth there, as Tennyson and his poems are a natural growth of those phases. It remains to be distinctly admitted that this man is a real first-class poet, infused amid all that ennui and aristocracy.[47]

Whitman was not alone in noting and deploring the ennui of the times. Arthur Henry Hallam observed that "the age in which we live comes late in our national progress. That first raciness and juvenile vigor of literature, when nature 'wantoned as in her prime, and played at will her virgin fancies' is gone, never to return. Since that day we have undergone a period of degradation."[48] In Whitman's eyes things could be far different in democratic America. On the western side of the Atlantic there had been no declension, no loss of vigor: "As if the opening of the western continent by discovery and what has transpired since in North and South America were less than the small theatre of the antique or the aimless sleep-walking of the middle ages!" (*LG 1855*, p. 6).[49]

Particularly in Tennyson, among English poets, ennui could be connected with a disproportionate emphasis on love. For Whitman, Tennyson

> is the bard of ennui and of the aristocracy, and their combination into love. This love is the old stock love of playwrights and romancers, Shakspere the same as the rest. It is possessed of the same unnatural and shocking passion for some girl or woman, that wrenches it from its manhood, emasculated and impotent, without strength to hold the rest of the objects and goods of life in their proper positions.
>   . . . [Tennyson and the people of the parlors] accept the love depicted in romances as the great business of a life or a poem, [and] both seem unconscious of the mighty truths of eternity and immortality.[50]

Like many of his eighteenth-century predecessors, Whitman felt both that the passion of love was given too large a place in literature and that the constant depiction of this passion contributed to effeminacy of character.[51] He felt that love as depicted in "romances" was false love; he called it elsewhere a "sickly scrofulous crude amorousness."[52] This outlook doubtless influenced Whitman's low opinion of some of Tennyson's poems.[53]

A preoccupation with love caused distortion by displacing other elements of life from their "proper positions"; a preoccupation with beauty caused a harmful restriction of the range of poetry. Of course Whitman himself was never blind to the need for beauty in poetry.[54] But, though he recognized its importance as an end product, he disagreed with those who limited poetic subject matter to beauty in the external world. Coleridge had written that "we must imitate nature! . . . the beautiful in nature." And Hallam had contended that "whenever the mind of the artist suffers itself to be occupied, during the period of creation, by any other predominant motive than the desire of beauty, the result is false in art."[55] In contrast, Whitman argues that those who confine themselves to the beautiful have become "confectioners and upholsterers of verse." Poets should instead encompass as much life as possible and reveal the beauty of all, especially the beauty of the common and average. As he notes in a nice paradox, "the law of the requisites of a grand poem . . . is originality, and the average and superb beauty of the ensemble."[56]

Polished and adorned poetry might suit the English and yet be wholly inappropriate for an American.[57] Whitman believed that, unlike its English equivalent, the American character was yet to be created. Perhaps this perception of a difference in stages of cultural development, one often accepted by English reviewers like Hallam, led him to be far more concerned with the needs of his audience than were many nineteenth-century English theorists. Of course the romantics held various opinions about the reader, and some poets, notably Blake and Wordsworth, did acknowledge the importance of the audience.[58] Nonetheless, many romantics adopted extreme theoretical positions that support M. H. Abrams's conclusion that there is "something singularly fatal to the audience in the romantic point of view." Shelley's nightingale "sings to cheer its own solitude"; Keats remarked that "I never wrote one single Line of Poetry with the least Shadow of public thought"; and John Stuart Mill viewed the poem as a soliloquy.[59] Whitman was always opposed to this tendency in romanticism. Even as early as the "albot Wilson" notebook, he strives to find a language that will reach and fully engage his audience: "The truths I tell to you or any other, may not be plain to you, because I do not translate them fully from my idiom into yours.—If I could do so, and do it well, they would be as apparent to you as they are to me; for they are truths.—No two have exactly the same language, and the great translator and joiner of the whole is the poet,[.] He has the divine grammar of all tongues" (*NUPM* 1:61). Reaching the people and being accepted by them was so important to Whitman that he made it the test of the poet.

There is a mystery in all of this. Somehow Whitman never seemed to doubt the intrinsic importance of his own way of approaching poetry. He was certain that poetry *must* reach the people and on their own terms. In fact, certainty was the major enabling factor in these first years of creativity. It allowed Whitman to contradict predecessors, to challenge convention, to stand alone in insistence on the democratic norm. It subsumed every difficulty in the name of assertion, innovation, and provocation.

Whitman's "Pictures" and Tennyson's "Palace of Art"

Tennyson emerged as Whitman's key rival among English poets, as is suggested by "An English and an American Poet." Whitman opposed the romantics; he vigorously debated Tennyson. Most previous discussions, if they mention English influence at all, have stressed the importance of Wordsworth and Shelley to Whitman. But the American poet was challenged and provoked more by an active rival than by near predecessors, more by the reigning laureate than by figures distanced by death, more by broad-scale disagreement than by any amount of agreement. Whitman's apprentice poem "Pictures" (probably composed in

1853 or 1854) suggests that Tennyson's "Palace of Art" was vitally important for Whitman's poetic development.[60] "Pictures" corresponds in so many ways to "The Palace of Art" that Whitman seems to speak back to Tennyson, creating a dialogue so sustained and edged as to all but eliminate the chance of coincidental parallels.

Whitman claimed repeatedly in 1855 that his work took "no hint" from other writers. Yet effective opposition requires knowledge, and it was Tennyson who represented to Whitman the quintessential "literary" figure of his time. The American saw great strengths and great weaknesses in his English counterpart: "Ulysses," he felt, "redeems a hundred 'Princesses' and 'Mauds' and shows the *Great Master*."[61] The early Whitman sought confrontation with Tennyson, and he chose as a target the Englishman's statement about social and intellectual principles, "The Palace of Art." In his marginalia, Whitman commented on two stanzas of this work (probably also registering his opinion of the whole): "Poorly done."[62]

"The Palace of Art" dramatizes a central problem for Tennyson, the conflict between private vision and social responsibility. The poem describes a Soul who decides to build for herself a palace of art filled with the materials of the imagination. She will withdraw into her fortress-like solitude out of an aristocratic disdain for humanity:

O God-like isolation which art mine,
    I can but count thee perfect gain,
What time I watch the darkening droves of swine
    That range on yonder plain.[63]

The Soul furnishes her luxurious palace with pictures drawn from a wide variety of human experience, including literature, art, religion, myth, and philosophy. The poem's climax is reached when the Soul enthrones herself only to discover that her splendid

rooms and isolation are intolerable. Remorseful, she returns to the
world of humanity and dwells in a cottage, although she leaves
her palace intact.

Modern critics often find the work—described by Tennyson
as "a sort of allegory"—to be flawed because it ultimately turns to
"sermonising."[64] Given the poet's stated purpose, to illustrate
that "the God-like life is with man and for man," many readers are
troubled by both the expansive accounts of the palace and the
poem's ending, which leaves open the possibility of an eventual
return to the palace.[65] Whatever his message, Tennyson displayed his attraction to aestheticism by devoting fifty-five stanzas
to the palace and one to the cottage in the vale.[66]

Whitman, shunning the ornate style of Tennyson, abandons
exotic wonders—the pyramids, the gardens of Babylon—in favor
of "a wonder beyond any of them, / Namely yourself—the form
and thoughts of a man." "Pictures" is composed of the images in
his own mind, his "little house," recollected from life and drawn
from reading in varied sources, including *A Few Days in Athens*,
Felton's *History of Greece*, geography and Egyptology books, the
Bible, and Homer.[67] Whitman follows Tennyson in employing the
central trope of the mind as a house or chamber and in treating his
subject matter pictorially.[68]

Whitman wrote the poem that Tennyson's thesis, if not his
temperament, called for. In general, Whitman comments on Tennyson by contradicting him. The opposition is clearest when the
two treat some of the same poets, including Dante and Shakespeare. Tennyson adorns the walls of one chamber in the palace
with portraits of Milton, Shakespeare, Dante, and Homer. The
highest honors are saved, however, for the "godlike faces of Plato
and Bacon." Having raised poets and philosophers to deities, the
Soul worships their images: "O silent faces of the Great and
Wise, / My Gods, with whom I dwell!"[69]

The reality of Whitman's pictures contrasts with the artificiality of Tennyson's art. Instead of glorifying the intellect and idolizing poets and philosophers, Whitman juxtaposes them with laborers and animals, including a Boston truckman and his "sagacious" horses.

> And here, see you—here walks the Boston truckman, by
>   the side of his string-team—see the three horses, pacing
>   stately, sagacious, one ahead of another;
> —And this—whose picture is this?
> Who is this, with rapid feet, curious, gay—going up and
>   down Mannahatta, through the streets, along the shores,
>   working his way through the crowds, observant and
>   singing?
> And this head of melancholy Dante, poet of penalties—
>   poet of hell;
> But this is a portrait of Shakespear, limner of feudal
>   European lords (here are my hands, my brothers—one
>   for each of you;)
> —And there are wood-cutters, cutting down trees in my
>   north east woods—see you, the axe uplifted;
> And that is a picture of a fish-market—see there the shad,
>   flat-fish, the large halibut,—there a pile of lobsters, and
>   there another of oysters;
> Opposite, a drudge in the kitchen, working, tired—and
>   there again the laborer, in stained clothes, sour-smelling,
>   sweaty—and again black persons and criminals;
> And there the frivolous person—and there a crazy
>   enthusiast—and there a young man lies sick of a fever,
>   and is soon to die;
> This, again, is a Spanish bull-fight—see, the animal with
>   bent head, fiercely advancing;
> And here, see you, a picture of a dream of despair, (—is it
>   unsatisfied love?)   [*CRE*, p. 645]

Rather than secluding himself in a rarefied setting, Whitman plunges insistently into the crowds, "going up and down Mannahatta." And instead of exhibiting what Joseph Sendry calls the "initial presumption" of Tennyson's poem—the Soul's belief that she is "worthy to dwell in the company of the greatest minds in the western world"—Whitman recognizes that Shakespeare and Dante have significance in human communities, not in a sequestered realm of art objects.[70] As Soule notes, Whitman seeks human contact, "not metaphors of learning or busts of famous figures."[71] Tennyson makes poets and philosophers distant gods; Whitman brings them close, makes them family.

Not surprisingly, the political implications of "The Palace of Art" and "Pictures" differ sharply. Tennyson suggested that revolution leads to anarchy:

> The people here, a beast of burden slow,
>   Toiled onward, pricked with goads and stings;
> Here played, a tiger, rolling to and fro
>   The heads and crowns of kings;
>
> Here rose, an athlete, strong to break or bind
>   All force in bonds that might endure,
> And here once more like some sick man declined,
>   And trusted any cure.[72]

In an apparent reference to the French Revolution, Tennyson indicates that rule by the people is dying. Whitman shows its vitality by presenting portraits of regicides and then examples of democracy in action: portraits of Thomas Jefferson compiling the Declaration of Independence, of Emerson lecturing at the lecturer's desk, and of Congress in session in the Capitol. The progression suggests that Jefferson the revolutionary helped set democracy in motion, Emerson sustains it, and Congress enacts it.

In "The Palace of Art," the Soul's distrust of people has sexual as well as political implications. The stanza following the celebration of her "God-like isolation" hints at a major reason for her withdrawal: "In filthy sloughs they roll a prurient skin, / They graze and wallow, breed and sleep." Fear of sexuality lies behind her choice of isolation; in fact, many of the impulses of the soul are not life-affirming at all. As W. David Shaw has observed, "a chill descends whenever we feel behind the poem Tennyson's desolate truth, that for the soul art has become, not an affair of life and people, but a tomb."[73]

Instead of choosing isolation to avoid carnality, Whitman makes sex the largest frame of "Pictures," the all-subsuming, all-justifying vital force. Using a common strategy in his poetry, he places the crucial remark in parentheses: "(The phallic choice of America leaves the finesse of cities, and all the returns of commerce or agriculture, and the magnitude of geography, and achievements of literature and art, and all the shows of exterior victory, to enjoy the breeding of full-sized men, or one full-sized man or woman, unconquerable and simple . . .)" (*CRE*, p. 648). Whitman's attempt to phallicize poetic discourse speaks to the gender issues involved with poetic identity. One critic has argued that Tennyson, "a gruff, very strong and masculine" individual, extended and completed himself "in the creation of the delicate, the fragile, the feminine."[74] The temptation is to conclude that these poets represent mirror images of one another, with Tennyson's largely masculine personality leading to a feminine poetry and Whitman's feminine sensibility leading to his "rough" pose and a masculine poetry. But the neat formulation oversimplifies Whitman in at least two important ways. First, masculine and feminine characteristics are thoroughly mixed in Whitman's poetry.[75] Second, the notion that poets achieve wholeness by complementing existing personality traits rests on an ahistorical psychological model.

The phallus was one subject that reputable art generally over-looked; for Whitman, the phallus served as a symbol for every-thing that was excluded and that he decided to speak for, every-thing thought too trivial or too low for "poetry." Whitman concludes that the problem of art is so acute that not new art but only anti-art can offset the false separation of art and life. The writing of "Pictures" pushed Whitman toward an extremely anti-poetic poetry. (Significantly, after "Pictures," Whitman men-tioned neither Dante nor Shakespeare nor any other predecessor in his poems until after the first three editions had been produced, until after the Civil War, and until after his abandonment of his role as a "rough.") During his "foreground," Whitman learned to define himself and his project through negation. His poetic inno-vations are not the devices of a splendid isolation so much as they are a series of ingenious counters to English practice.

 CHAPTER TWO

"Strangle the singers who will not sing
you loud and strong"
Whitman and Emerson Reconsidered

Paradoxically, although Whitman's relation to literary tradition as a whole has been insufficiently studied, his indebtedness to Emerson has been repeatedly discussed
and frequently overemphasized. Edward Shils, in *Tradition*, suggests why a person such as Whitman might benefit from an Emerson. Shils's example comes from politics, but the passage is worth
quoting because it explains why so much of the Whitman-Emer-
son criticism has been mistaken in its emphases:

> A person not hitherto a socialist becomes a socialist not pri-
> marily because he has thought it all out for himself but be-
> cause, having certain inclinations of the mind, e.g., an aver-
> sion to poverty or a dislike of egoistic hedonism or of the
> power which is connected with the private ownership of
> property, his mind inclines or is disposed in the direction set
> by experience and sentiment, toward general beliefs acquired
> from tradition. . . . The person so disposed finds ready to
> hand a more differentiated picture and a more differentiated

plan already in being. This picture and this plan are intellectual traditions. He becomes a possession as well as a pos-
sessor of the tradition.

Shils points out that if the individual is "very imaginative, curious, ratiocinative, and studious," he will modify the picture and
plan to suit his own intellectual and moral powers. But if he is
weak intellectually, he will accept it without alteration, to the
extent that he can assimilate it; "he will add nothing to it, he might
even simplify and impoverish the tradition of the idea or complex
of ideas which he receives."[1]

Most critics depict a Whitman more possessed by than in
possession of the Emersonian tradition. Yvor Winters argues that
Whitman merely adopted Emerson's ideas: "I must ask my readers
to accept on faith, until they find it convenient to check the matter,
the generally accepted view that the main ideas of Whitman are
identical with those of Emerson." F. O. Matthiessen holds a similar view: the "whole question of the relation of Whitman's theory
and practice of art to Emerson's is fascinating since, starting from
similar if not identical positions they end up with very different
results." Hyatt Waggoner asserts that "The Poet" contains "nearly all the ideas Whitman was later to express in his poetry." And
Albert Gelpi believes that Whitman cast himself "almost point for
point . . . in the role Emerson had proclaimed."[2]

These and other sensitive and knowledgeable critics have
drawn primarily on two sources of evidence: Whitman's numerous echoes of Emerson, particularly in the 1855 *Leaves of Grass*, and
Whitman's own statements of indebtedness from the 1856 open
letter, including this remark to the "Master": "Those shores you
found. I say you have led The States there—have led Me there"
(*CRE*, p. 739). Such evidence has led to enormous emphasis on
this relationship (often, as Jerome Loving has pointed out, with a

pro-Emerson bias).[3] Yet if we take Emerson as Whitman's single master, if we conclude, as Harold Bloom has, that Whitman displays a "primal fixation upon Emerson," we have to ignore other signals. Whitman's praise of Emerson is usually undercut or otherwise qualified. And, despite his own claims to the contrary, he is receptive to a wide range of influences beyond Emerson. If Emerson is "Master," what are we to make of Tennyson, the *Great Master*," or of Whitman himself, "a master after my own kind"?[4]

To illuminate the key years in the relationship between Emerson and Whitman—1855 and 1856—we can begin by examining Whitman's open letter to Emerson, included as an appendix to the second edition of *Leaves of Grass*. My reading of the letter opposes nearly every other critical assessment. By grasping what Whitman thought was at issue in the relationship in 1856, we may be better able to evaluate Emerson's contribution to the achievement of 1855. The "master" letter clarifies the nature of Whitman's accomplishment, indebtedness, and purposes in the most productive period of his career.

The complicated 1856 letter, usually taken to be a straightforward statement of indebtedness, does not sustain interpretations of the Emerson-Whitman connection as a master-disciple relationship. The letter has received partial readings that typically focus on what have been called "mawkish" passages and ignore strong subversive elements in the letter.[5] A more complex reading of the letter would follow its labyrinthian course, noting the careening movements, observing the violent imagery, evaluating the purposeful offensiveness of the letter in light of an overall relationship that was anything but untroubled.

It is important to recall what preceded the letter. The 1855 *Leaves of Grass* asserted a myth of total independence from other writers. Yet, as his marginalia shows and "Pictures" suggests, Whitman attained an independent artistic maturity partly as a result of having passed through so much during the 1840s and early 1850s, including Emersonianism. Before he wrote *Leaves of Grass*, he had heard Emerson lecture, read his essays, and adopted some of his language and ideas. Yet by 1855 Whitman perceived, as he would later say, that Emersonianism "breeds the giant that destroys itself" (*PW* 2:517–18). An intense attachment to Emersonianism in the early 1850s (manifested in "Pictures" by his vignette of Emerson), gave way as early as the first edition to serious misgivings about Emerson and a larger need to reject *all* models. Thus he was determined, as he noted in his anonymous reviews, to make a "new school" and to "set models" rather than follow those of others; "not a whisper comes out of him of the old stock talk and rhyme of poetry" because other writers "do not seem to have touched him."[6] Whitman was both denying influences and glorying in his own power to transmute literary materials so as to make them his own. His commentary on *Leaves* scorned all previous poets, including Emerson, for they seemed to be followers unable to achieve a native independence. "English versification is full of these danglers, and America follows after them. Everybody writes poetry, and yet there is not a single poet."[7]

Whitman had enormous expectations for the 1855 edition, yet his book attracted little positive response, leaving him under intense psychic pressure. Central questions of identity were interwoven in the metamorphosis from Walter Whitman into Walt Whitman, a change that coincided with the death of his father, Walter Whitman, Sr. The reviews of *Leaves of Grass*—largely negative, some brutally harsh—were countered by Emerson's marvelous letter praising "the most extraordinary piece of wit and wisdom America has yet contributed." The temptation to return to a father-figure was great, particularly to one who was supportive during this reception crisis. Thus, following the death in 1855 of Walter Whitman, Sr., and his own attacks on poetic fathers, he experienced a troubling uneasiness, even guilt. Emerson's praise greeting him at the beginning of a great career was at the same time exhilarating and discomfiting, since it came from a benefactor he had denied. Thus, Whitman's grandiose claims of total independence made in 1855 received tortured reconsideration only a year later.

The poet shifted his position in a very complicated way. Intending to deflect harsh criticism by relying on a pure and honored authority, he hoped, in ostensibly affirming the Emerson connection, to reinforce and publicize a strong endorsement of *Leaves*. No longer overtly claiming to be the fountainhead of tradition, he gives this role (in some places in the letter) to Emerson: "Those shores you found. I say you have led The States there— have led Me there. I say that none has ever done, or ever can do, a greater deed for The States, than your deed. Others may line out the lines, build cities, work mines, break up farms; it is yours to have been the original true Captain who put to sea, intuitive, positive, rendering the first report, to be told less by any report, and more by the mariners of a thousand bays, in each tack of their arriving and departing, many years after you" (*CRE*, p. 739). Here Whitman sounds as if tradition works through the kind teachings of a "master" or the heroic guidance of a "captain" showing the way. These metaphors suggest a relatively easy and painless transmission of ideas and inspiration.

Yet the letter puts forth various ideas about literary tradition, many of which emphasize rupture and difference more than continuity. He called for "revolutionists" to advance, "sweeping off the swarms of routine representatives, officers in power, bookmakers" (*CRE*, p. 734). Whitman argues that the essential act for American artists is not to find a master but to walk "freely out from the old traditions": "Poets here, literats here, are to rest on organic different bases from other countries; not a class set apart, circling only in the circle of themselves, modest and pretty, desperately scratching for rhymes, pallid with white paper, shut off, aware of the old pictures and traditions of the race, but unaware of the actual race around them—not breeding in and in among each other till they all have the scrofula. Lands of ensemble, bards of ensemble! Walking freely out from the old traditions, as our politics has walked out" (CRE, p. 736). Because American poets "recognize nothing behind them superior to what is present with them," they possess a "spirit that will be nothing less than master." It would be hard to find another follower who so stressed the importance of being "master."

Could Whitman have had Emerson in mind when he spoke of "routine representatives" and "old traditions" linked to "other countries"? Quite possibly. The 1856 letter begins and ends by acknowledging Emerson's authority only to call that authority into question. The letter thanks Emerson by acknowledging a genuine debt to an intellectual forerunner and catalyst, but it also defines the limits of that debt. Whitman purposefully thanked Emerson in a way so outlandish that it accentuated the differences between them. Emerson may have helped bring Whitman to a boil, but Whitman bubbled over with all-inclusive condemnations: what are we to think of Emerson when Whitman criticizes *all* American poets as pedants and eunuchs, quiet snifflers who deny the place of sex in literature?[8] What has become of Emerson when Whitman chastises American writers in the following manner: "There is no great author. . . . None believes in These States. . . . Not a man faces round" (CRE, pp. 734–35)? These condemnations deliberately include all predecessors, none excluded. Moreover, Whitman first labels Emerson the "master" and then pointedly and consistently calls for new masters to replace the old. In the same letter Whitman creates and subverts a master-disciple relationship with Emerson.

Whitman also frequently turned the word "master" in unexpected directions. Granted: at a surface level, Whitman takes the role of follower, perhaps intending to evoke from readers

thoughts of Plato learning from Socrates or Dante learning from Virgil. But inherent in the teacher-student relationship is the possibility that the student will somehow surpass the teacher. At the same time, Whitman draws on other, less positive, connotations of the word "master." In antebellum America the word was used in connection with hierarchical conditions: the master-apprentice relationship Whitman was familiar with in New York and the master-slave relationship that engaged him as journalist and poet. The use of the word "overseer" in the 1856 letter, the violence of Whitman's language, and the psychology of the relationship combine to suggest the master-slave trope.

The choice of the word "master" to evoke an enslaving presence is not surprising, given the context of 1856. He heard much abolitionist rhetoric claiming that "the slaves were to their masters as the Americans had been to the British."[9] Moreover, he saw the economic position of his class threatened by changing market conditions and by slavery.[10] The poet did not employ casually the language of masters and slaves, hierarchy and equality—these matters were central to his thought. Whitman began his poetic career even as his country lurched toward self-destruction over these issues. His first notebook lines in the manner of *Leaves* declared:

I am the poet of slaves and of the masters of slaves
I am the poet of the body
And I am

I am the poet of the body
And I am the poet of the soul
I go with the slaves of the earth equally with the masters
And I will stand between the masters and the slaves,
Entering into both so that both shall understand me alike.

[*NUPM* 1:67]

The 1856 letter vacillates between a master-disciple and a master-slave relationship. With the exception of the introduction and the conclusion, the letter displays the psychodynamics of a master-slave relationship in the desire for a reversal in the power relationship. The movement of the letter has Whitman first submitting, then dominating, then submitting again, as he moves back and forth in uneasy, unstable role-shifting. That his key term would be "master" is not surprising, given that the slavery question and the dignity of white labor were fundamental to the conception of the first *Leaves* and to his conception of American character. He asked in a notebook: "What real Americans can be made out of slaves? What real Americans can be made out of the masters of slaves?"[11]

Whitman's "real Americans," all evidence suggests, would discover divinity in the average and would oppose special privilege. From the 1840s to the 1890s, and with increasing point over the years, Whitman stressed class differences when discussing Emerson. Emerson's remarks in his journals warrant this criticism: "The worst of charity, is, that the lives you are asked to preserve are not worth preserving. The calamity is the masses."[12] David Leverenz points out that for Emerson laborers are "the herd, the mob, the mass, 'bugs and spawn,' at best a kind of larva."[13] Whitman objected to an elitism tantamount to a breach of democratic faith. His approach was utterly different: "Every day I go among the people of Manhattan Island, Brooklyn, and other cities, and among the young men, to discover the spirit of them, and to refresh myself" (*CRE*, pp. 731–32).

The 1856 letter implicates Emerson in perpetuating a foreign spirit and associates Emerson with European and especially English culture. The early Whitman insists repeatedly that the way of the "gentleman" violates the spirit of America: "[A]ll our intellectual people . . . dress by London and Paris modes . . .

obey the authorities. . . . One sees unmistakably genteel persons, travelled, college-learned, used to be served by servants, conversing without heat or vulgarity . . . walking through handsomely carpeted parlors. . . . Where in America is the first show of America?"[14] As George H. Soule has noted, "Whitman laments the influence of Tennyson's spirit on American culture, characterizing the young men of the United States as 'a parcel of helpless dandies, who can neither fight, work, shoot, ride, run, command' because they have followed fashionable European modes [models] rather than the 'popular substratum' of their own nation."[15] Of course, the overall accusation is at least as old as Royall Tyler's in *The Contrast* (1787), but it shows once again Whitman's facility in turning established strands of thought to new uses.

Whitman had reason to associate Emerson with English literature. Emerson, of course, called for independence from the courtly muses and seemed to endorse an oppositional approach by demanding that Americans be their own masters. Yet he was ambiguous on English literature; his friendly allusions to English writers suggested that he regarded himself as working within the English tradition. Moreover, in 1852 Emerson observed in his journal, "We are the heir . . . we are the Englishman, by gravitation by destiny, & the laws of the Universe . . . we are the lawful son." And in *English Traits* (1856) he observed, "The American is only the continuation of English genius into new conditions."[16] Emerson's own complex attitude toward America's European heritage—his vacillations between calls for independence and remarks of reverence—contributed to Whitman's characteristic ambivalence in his acceptance of the "master."

Whereas Emerson thought of the American as the "lawful son" of the English, Whitman thought that English-American unions typically produced "false heirs." His discussion of the

English heritage—a notable part of the letter to Emerson—displays the same dizzying movement as the larger discussion of master-follower relationships. What begins as "generous praise" ends in violent sexual imagery of submission and domination:

> What else can happen The States, even in their own despite? That huge English flow, so sweet, so undeniable, has done incalculable good here, and is to be spoken of for its own sake with generous praise and with gratitude. Yet the price The States have had to lie under for the same has not been a small price. Payment prevails; a nation can never take the issues of the needs of other nations for nothing. America, grandest of lands . . . collapses quick as lightning at the repeated, admonishing, stern, words, Where are any mental expressions from you, beyond what you have copied or stolen? . . . You are young, have the perfectest of dialects. . . . As justice has been strictly done to you, from this hour do strict justice to yourself. Strangle the singers who will not sing you loud and strong. Open the doors of The West. Call for new great masters to comprehend new arts, new perfections, new wants. Submit to the most robust bard till he remedy your barrenness. Then you will not need to adopt the heirs of others; you will have true heirs, begotten of yourself, blooded with your own blood. [*CRE*, p. 732]

The extremism of this passage suggests that the poet is concerned with more than literary independence. Perhaps what Robert Duncan has called a "homosexuality in distress" can be heard here.[17] Because of Whitman's sexual orientation, he faced a childless future; yet as the poet of sex, it was extremely important to him not to be barren.

The preceding chapter noted that Whitman chided Tennyson for being "emasculated and impotent." Similar language is used in the open letter, strengthening the association between Emerson and the English: "There is no great author; every one has demeaned himself to some etiquette or impotence. There is no manhood or life-power in poems; there are shoats and geldings more like. Or literature will be dressed up, a fine gentleman, distasteful to our instincts, foreign to our soil. Its neck bends right and left wherever it goes. Its costumes and jewelry prove how little it knows Nature. Its flesh is soft; it shows less and less of the indefinable hard something that is Nature" (*CRE*, p. 734). Writing to the author of *Nature*, Whitman insists that American authors have proven how little they know nature. A reliance on aesthetic refinements has led, he suggests, to effeminate poetry. Opposing a "fine gentleman," "foreign" influence, and flaccid accounts of nature, Whitman offered a "new manhood or life-power in poems."

What conditions could have produced such a letter? Emerson was initially an enabler, as is suggested by "Pictures" and the echoes of "The Poet" found throughout the 1855 *Leaves of Grass*. Whitman responded to this predecessor with exhilaration in the early 1850s because of the American possibilities he outlined in the face of English excellence. Emerson spoke to Whitman's concerns: the question of how to deal with the English, the question of manliness, the question of the colossal cipher or the remaking of the self. Yet as early as the first edition Whitman began to turn away—partly because *that* was Emersonian, partly because the more he pondered Emerson the more ambivalent he became about the political and poetical implications of his version of manliness, his social outlook, and his attitude toward foreign inheritance.

This problematic side of the 1856 letter directly informs "Song of Myself" and makes it a very different poem from the one Whitman scholarship usually gives us (outpourings of an "Emerson with a body").[18] "Song of Myself," broadly autobiographical in shape, should be regarded as an allegory of the imagination.[19] Whitman's inquiry, his self-wrestling, his astonishing insights and puzzling discoveries all move him in the direction of a mature independence incompatible with the role he later adopts of disciple. "Song of Myself" enacts the discovery of independence through its treatment, most notably, of the common man and sexuality. Whitman also registers his struggle with Emerson: his treatment of particulars in his poem builds on—and frequently turns against—Emersonian suggestions. This pattern of indebtedness and resistance deserves closer attention.

Comparing the visionary experiences of Emerson and Whitman is revealing. In *Nature*, Emerson describes himself standing on bare ground, looking into infinite space. Then, characteristically, he turns to spirit: "all mean egotism vanishes. I become a transparent eyeball; I am nothing; I see all; the currents of Universal Being circulate through me."[20] For the Emersonian poet, experience is etherealized as it is filtered through the intellect. The epiphany, a cerebral event, underscores Emerson's discomfort with intimacy, his distrust of the body. Here, as in "The Poet," he glorifies "the centrifugal tendency of a man" to seek "passage out into that free space . . . to escape the custody of that body in which he is pent up, and of that jail yard of individual relations in which he is enclosed."[21]

For Whitman, no better way can be found to describe the nature of his vision than to employ sexual metaphors:

Loafe with me on the grass . . . . loose the stop from your throat,
Not words, not music or rhyme I want . . . . not custom or lecture, not even the best,
Only the lull I like, the hum of your valved voice.

I mind how we lay in June, such a transparent summer morning;

You settled your head athwart my hips and gently turned
　　over upon me,
And parted the shirt from my bosom-bone, and plunged
　　your tongue to my barestript heart,
And reached till you felt my beard, and reached till you
　　held my feet.

                                        [LG 1855, pp. 28–29]

Although some claim that Whitman took his idea of the soul from
Emerson, his early poems emphasize what Emerson dismissed
from importance: the soul's medium is the body. Emerson laments the custody of flesh; Whitman celebrates the body and in
particular sexual arousal, for he links it with the active imagination.[22]

The insights reached after Emerson and Whitman's epi-
phanies are quite different. Whitman's litany leads to a doctrine of
love:

Swiftly arose and spread around me the peace and joy and
　　knowledge that pass all the art and argument of the
　　earth;
And I know that the hand of God is the elderhand of my
　　own,
And I know that the spirit of God is the eldest brother of
　　my own,
And that all the men ever born are also my
　　brothers . . . . and the women my sisters and lovers,
And that a kelson of the creation is love;
And limitless are leaves stiff or drooping in the fields.
And brown ants in the little wells beneath them,
And mossy scabs of the wormfence, and heaped stones,
　　and elder and mullen and pokeweed.

                                        [LG 1855, p. 29]

Against Emerson's claim that "the soul knows no persons," Whitman stressed personality and an identified soul. Recasting Emerson's impersonal deity, Whitman makes the Universal Being into "a loving bedfellow," a dispenser of letters, grassy handkerchiefs, and plentiful baskets.[23]

Emerson welcomed isolation and the abandonment of all creatures as a route for spiritual development. But this path in no way appealed to Whitman, so needing friendship and so anchored in the body.[24] After the transparent eyeball experience, Emerson develops this credo: "The name of the nearest friend sounds then foreign and accidental: to be brothers, to be acquaintances, master or servant, is then a trifle and disturbance. I am the lover of uncontained and immortal beauty."[25] His experience diminishes rather than extends his sense of human community: he loves "uncontained and immortal beauty"—not people and not Whitman's "brown ants" and "mossy scabs of the wormfence."

Whitman, disdaining rivalry with Emerson and other poets, stresses at the outset of "Song of Myself" the challenge offered by the much more formidable force of the sun:

> The feeling of health . . . . the full-noon trill . . . . the song
>   of me rising from bed and *meeting the sun*.
> . . . .
>
> Stop this day and night with me and you shall possess the
>   origin of all poems,
> You shall possess the good of the earth and sun . . . . there
>   are millions of suns left,
> You shall no longer take things at second or third
>   hand . . . . nor look through the eyes of the
>   dead . . . . nor feed on the spectres in books.
>   [*LG 1855*, p. 26; emphasis added]

That the sun, the generative life force of nature, is both Whitman's defense (against other poets) and his most potent challenger had been suggested earlier in the 1855 Preface in his discussion of mastery and the "grandeur of the wildest fury of the elements." There is "something in the soul," he claims, "which says, Rage on, Whirl on, I tread master here and everywhere, Master of the spasms of the sky and shatter of the sea, Master of nature and passion and death, And of all terror and all pain." To master the cosmos is to be above poetic squabbling, as the next sentence in the Preface asserts: "The American bards shall be marked for generosity and affection and for encouraging competitors" (*LG 1855*, pp. 13–14). Belying his claim to support rivals, Whitman disqualifies or at least trivializes other poets when he promises access to the good of the sun, whereas others provide only "spectres in books." In this self-aggrandizing myth, Whitman is the source; others are shadows. Whitman speaks as the origin; others offer second- or third-hand accounts.

Near the midpoint of "Song of Myself," Whitman returns to the interconnected concerns raised by the sun and the master, and by earliness and belatedness, in a pair of remarkable passages that bring together the full implications of Whitman's generative imagery. He presents himself as the vehicle of a new order of creation as he joins human creativity, expressed through sexuality, and nature's creativity, empowered by the sun, in images that describe the engendering of a new poetic order.

> To behold the daybreak!
> The little light fades the immense and diaphanous
>   shadows,
> The air tastes good to my palate.
>
> Hefts of the moving world at innocent gambols, silently
>   rising, freshly exuding,
> Scooting obliquely high and low.
>
> Something I cannot see puts upward libidinous prongs,
> Seas of bright juice suffuse heaven.

> The earth by the sky staid with . . . . the daily close of their
>   junction,
> The heaved challenge from the east that moment over my
>   head,
> The mocking taunt, See then whether you shall be master!
>
> [*LG 1855*, p. 50]

After promising to give us "the good of the earth and sun" and indicating that "a kelson of the creation is love," the poet, himself a universal lover, describes the love-making of the earth and sun. This section names the poet for the first time—"Walt Whitman, an American, one of the roughs, a kosmos" (*LG 1855*, p. 48)—and, in the lines that follow, answers the jeering challenge of the sun by indicating that this name is inseparable from mastery.

> Dazzling and tremendous how quick the sunrise would kill
>   me,
> If I could not now and always send sunrise out of me.
>
> We also ascend dazzling and tremendous as the sun,
> We found our own my soul in the calm and cool of the
>   daybreak.
>
> My voice goes after what my eyes cannot reach,
> With the twirl of my tongue I encompass worlds and
>   volumes of worlds.
>
> [*LG 1855*, p. 50]

Whitman contends that the rising sun would master him if the sun were a *solitary* prime mover and if he could not ascend in an equally radiant fashion. (For Whitman, to be the Sun was to preclude the possibility of being Emerson's son.) The mention of "We found our own my soul" at daybreak refers back, of course, to the transparent summer morning when "I" and the "soul" reached a perfect unity in section five. Now Whitman's voice, empowered

WHITMAN AND EMERSON RECONSIDERED

by the tongue plunged to the heart in section five, encompasses "volumes of worlds"—both many worlds and many books. The poet claims to match the original prime mover with a casual twirl of his tongue. Later in the poem he returns to his competition with the sun: "Flaunt of the sunshine I need not your bask . . . . lie over, / You light surfaces only . . . . I force the surfaces and the depths also" (*LG 1855*, p. 70). The exuberance and sheer audacity of Whitman's claims result from both the giddiness provoked by his early sense of his own artistic gift and a complex defensive reaction to Emerson and other poetic predecessors.

Whitman consistently associates himself with primal sources of energy and associates other poets with the lack of such energy. In the letter to Emerson, Whitman asked "Where is a savage and luxuriant man?" In "Song of Myself" Whitman makes it clear that he identifies *himself* with the savage whose words are "simple as grass" and who is precivilized yet modern. Indeed, the portrait of the savage captures the riddle of Whitman:

> Slowstepping feet and the common features, and the
>   common modes and emanations,
> They descend in new forms from the tips of his fingers.
>   [*LG 1855*, p. 70]

Out of the common, the savage (or Whitman) produces "new forms." The savage is a projection of the Real Me, incorporating Whitman's belief that his role in culture is to help shape the national identity. He is, after all, his own kind of master: "The friendly and flowing savage . . . . Who is he? / Is he waiting for civilization or past it and mastering it?" (*LG 1855*, p. 69). He offers his "eleves" an embodiment in language of "manhood, balanced, florid and full." He thereby provides a democratic equivalent of the role filled historically by hierarchies of priests.[26]

When Whitman discusses the cultural function of poetry, he

approaches it indirectly. He clearly imagines himself in section forty-six as a special type of leader rather than a follower. The entire poem has progressed toward these lines:

> I have no chair, nor church nor philosophy;
> I lead no man to a dinner-table or library or exchange,
> But each man and each woman of you I lead upon a knoll.
>
> [LG 1855, p. 80]

Throughout this section the problem is not that Whitman needs to free himself from timid discipleship; instead, he is concerned to free others from timidity.

> Long have you timidly waded, holding a plank by the shore,
> Now I will you to be a bold swimmer,
> To jump off in the midst of the sea, and rise again and nod to me and shout, and laughingly dash with your hair.
>
> [LG 1855, p. 81]

Whitman conceives of his "eleves" as equals. What difference exists between them stems from varying levels of development.

Like Emerson, Whitman understood the potentially destructive nature of the teacher-disciple relationship: "He most honors my style who learns under it to destroy the teacher" (LG 1855, p. 81). After writing "Song of Myself," for Whitman to return to the role of student or follower or disciple was to violate the persona he had created and to invite a poetic identity crisis. That such a crisis occurred seems clear from the fascinating and powerful but deeply self-divided quality of Whitman's 1856 letter to the "master." The nature of Whitman's own discovered creativity and an honest recognition of his differences with Emerson had earlier forced a break with his major American predecessor, a break first dramatized in "Song of Myself."

CHAPTER THREE

"Taking all hints to use them"

The Artistry of *Leaves of Grass*

The success of Whitman's pose as a "rough" can be measured by the many studies that ignore his resourcefulness in drawing on the leading poets of his era. Although his debt to Emerson's poetic theory is routinely noted, critics often implicitly endorse the largest part of Whitman's claim that he bore no resemblance to the "great past poets, or the later ones of England, such as Tennyson or Browning; or those of our own country, Bryant, Emerson, or Longfellow."[1] Whitman's many denials of literary indebtedness notwithstanding, a careful study of individual poems indicates that he absorbed much from his poetic contemporaries and romantic predecessors. Noting how he benefited from particular poets at different stages in his career provides an index to the changes in his poetic style, his poetic purposes, and his understanding of his audience.

Looking back at the 1855 edition, we may wonder why Whitman thought he could achieve any degree of popular success. His book, purged of the obvious allusions, shunned all familiar marks of poetry of the time. The radical experiments in form, the challenges to widely held values, the intellectual daring, and the hidden, complex meanings made *Leaves of Grass* ideally suited for unpopularity. C. Carroll Hollis has asserted, correctly, that Whitman's "true audience" was the "disaffected yet educated middle class reader who might be sympathetic and responsive to a radical new democratic poetry."[2] But though we can now see that this was the audience he realistically could seek, the poet thought otherwise and held the broadest aspirations. Whitman sought the double victory of both an enormous readership and the critical acclaim achieved by such poets as Longfellow and Tennyson. In his 1856 letter to Emerson, he marveled at journalism and other popular forms: "What a progress popular reading and writing has made in fifty years! What a progress fifty years hence!" (*CRE*, p. 733). These hopes are integrally related to his extraordinary claims for *Leaves of Grass:* "The way is clear to me. A few years and the average annual call for my Poems is ten or twenty thousand copies—more quite likely. Why should I hurry or compromise?" (*CRE*, p. 731).

It is important to avoid concluding that Whitman was either disingenuous or hopelessly naive about the chances of broad popular support for American art. By 1850, ninety percent of adult whites in the United States could read and write, making up the largest literate public in history.[3] The artist's situation remained open-ended, since the size of the possible audience for serious literature was yet unknown. The writers of the American Renaissance who came to maturity in the 1840s and 1850s had absorbed the heady atmosphere of the 1830s, when a variety of literary nationalists predicted that an enlightened popular audience would be responsive to American literary excellence. The literary market did expand rapidly after 1840 because of new social developments that encouraged reading: improved distribution of

books and periodicals brought by better roads and extended post-
al routes; new technological advances, such as the cylinder press,
which allowed publishers to produce books at reduced prices;
and the new organization of work and gender roles resulting
from "insurgent middle-class domesticity."[4] If such writers as
Hawthorne and Whitman could have foreseen what modern readers accept as a given—the rift between popular and critical taste—
they might have been less dismayed by their commercial failures.
What made such prescience virtually impossible was the example
of artists who did reach the public without lowering their standards. Emerson, for instance, was a welcome lecturer in hamlets
and cities across the land. Poe achieved popular and critical success overnight with "The Raven." And that unorthodox Englishman Martin Farquhar Tupper demonstrated that even an experimental verse form—similar to the one Whitman developed—
could contribute to success culminating in a triumphant tour of
America and dinner at the White House. In such a context, Whitman's early contention that "the proof of a poet" is in his reception becomes more understandable.

Although Whitman desired the recognition widely read poets
received, he did not approve uniformly of their poetic methods.
The Whitman of 1855 and 1856 admired Tennyson's "Ulysses"
but otherwise rejected his major English counterpart. Still, Tennyson's achievement was enviable: he reached the people, in-
trigued critical reviewers, and exercised a public role. As suggested in chapter one, Whitman revealed much about his own
allegiances when he attacked Tennyson and his followers in an
1855 review as "jinglers and snivellers and fops."[5] (In the 1840s
and 1850s reviewers described Poe, Longfellow, and Lowell as
American followers of Tennyson.)[6] Whitman's opposition to
what seemed destined to become the dominant poetic mode of his
age and his own rebellious example of poetry shorn of decorative,

melodious lyricism reveal his sympathy with a slightly earlier period, when Wordsworth was the major influence on American
poetry. Though sometimes critical of Wordsworth, Whitman
could nonetheless profit from his followers Bryant and Emerson
and from the Wordsworthian heritage of nature poetry and
non-"poetic" language.[7] Beginning in 1859, however, with the
first publication of "Out of the Cradle Endlessly Rocking," he
displayed a growing tendency to absorb characteristics of Ten-
nysonian verse and to achieve poetic effects akin to those he had
earlier denounced. His work became more obviously ornate, musical, and "poetic." He used apostrophes and invocations, he
developed a strong attachment to the incantatory use of words,
and he even began to make unmistakable allusions to poems by
Longfellow and Tennyson. Whitman's career began with its roots
largely hidden but nonetheless nourished by a Wordsworth-
Bryant-Emerson tradition. Later, as the next chapter indicates,
when he sought new ways to reach a broad audience, Whitman
grafted on the techniques of Tennyson and Longfellow.

"Peering, absorbing, translating": The Early
Whitman Engages His Predecessors

Bryant's influence on Whitman began with the pre-*Leaves* poetry. Whitman admired Bryant's role as a poet-journalist, contributed poems to his newspaper, and shared his general political
outlook. Bryant's popularity was such that by the 1840s "no poet
was read more eagerly."[8] Thus for Whitman, who would later
assert that in America a "bard is to be commensurate with a people," Bryant's extensive audience served as an important model of
the cultural impact a serious poet could have. In fact, "Thanatopsis" became so widely known and regularly imitated that it contributed to a popular aesthetic which associated the true sublime

with graveyard poetry.[9] Walter Whitman wrote in accord with this aesthetic in his earliest published poem, "Our Future Lot" (1838), echoing lines and phrases from "Thanatopsis." During the period of his early verse, he drew repeatedly on "Thanatopsis" and less eminent graveyard poems in "The Winding-Up," "The Love That is Hereafter," "Ambition," and "Death of the Nature-Lover."[10]

After his apprentice years, Whitman created two additional—and far greater—works largely inspired by "Thanatopsis." Whitman's treatment of death in "To Think of Time," the third poem of the 1855 *Leaves of Grass*, follows Bryant by offering consolation through a social vision. In the "Slowmoving and black lines" of the burial processions that go "ceaselessly over the earth" file Northerners and Southerners, people from the Atlantic and Pacific coasts and all areas between and beyond. Whitman's stress on the enormity of time and space reminds one of Bryant's ability to reach for dimension. For both poets, the vast natural world and the complex social world proceed with an appalling indifference after an individual's death. Yet as Robert A. Ferguson has pointed out, Bryant formulated an ultimately reassuring statement, a statement that draws much of its force from its political orientation: "There is a striking democracy in Bryant's society of the dead that owes much to republican instincts. The dead kings and patriarchs of the New World are the anachronisms of forgotten and lesser civilizations. But lying now in equality alongside matrons, maids, and speechless babes, they strangely prefigure and now corroborate the republican values of a more progressive era within 'the long train of ages.'"[11] Whitman's vision of death goes beyond Bryant's democracy by being radically democratic. Whereas the emphasis in "Thanatopsis" is on the nobility of the world-tomb (containing "the wise, the good / Fair forms and hoary seers of ages past"), Whitman insists on taking "strict account of all":

> The great masters and kosmos are well as they go . . . . the
>   heroes and good-doers are well,
> The known leaders and inventors and the rich owners and
>   pious and distinguished may be well,
> But there is more account than that . . . . there is strict
>   account of all.
>
> The interminable hordes of the ignorant and wicked are not
>   nothing,
> The barbarians of Africa and Asia are not nothing,
> The common people of Europe are not nothing . . . . the
>   American aborigines are not nothing,
> A zambo or a foreheadless Crowfoot or a Camanche is not
>   nothing,
> The infected in the immigrant hospital are not
>   nothing . . . . the murderer or mean person is not
>   nothing,
> The perpetual succession of shallow people are not nothing
>   as they go,
> The prostitute is not nothing . . . . the mocker of religion is
>   not nothing as he goes.
>
> > [*LG 1855*, p. 103]

Whitman explored the full implications of a society of the dead,
realizing that such a society would be filled with people of apparently little consequence, the "ignorant and wicked." Bryant's reassuring theme had been turned into a challenge: to accept Whitman's vision, to grasp that *all* people matter. In fact, Whitman
goes beyond human inclusiveness to argue that "every thing has
an eternal soul," even the trees, "rooted in the ground" and "the
weeds of the sea."

Whitman may have thought he could reach a broad audience,
despite the complexity of his thought, because his language ap-

proximates speech. Yet his transformation of speech into verse
was too revolutionary to be popular. Again the contrast with
Bryant is revealing. Both "Thanatopsis" and "To Think of Time"
are strikingly oratorical in tone. But Bryant's poem achieves this
tone through relatively standard means: he structures his poem
like a sermon, addressing his readers directly and exhorting them
in the introduction and the conclusion. Whitman seeks audience
involvement by addressing questions directly to "you" the reader
in second-person pronominal form. (In "To Think of Time" six-
teen of the nineteen questions are asked directly of "you," the
audience.)[12] The poem also displays other techniques unusual
enough to unsettle any audience Whitman could have imagined.
In the extended passage quoted above ("The great masters and
kosmos are well as they go"), Whitman makes extensive use of the
double negative, a feature common enough in conversation but
highly unusual in poetry. This brilliant poetic maneuver fits the
daring language of one who could ask bluntly "Have you dreaded
those earth-beetles?" and who faces but finally denies the possibility that all things could come but to "ashes of dung."

Whitman probably gave away more copies of the 1855 *Leaves*
than he sold. Nonetheless, he was buoyed by Emerson's admiring
letter, and in 1856 he printed one thousand copies of the second
edition and stereotyped the pages, apparently in expectation of
additional printings.[13] In one of his new poems, "This Compost,"
he again drew on Bryant's masterpiece in a highly original manner. He dealt with what had become a popular theme in an un-
popular, challenging, and incisive way. "This Compost" begins
precisely where "Thanatopsis" left off. Bryant urged his readers,
when confronted with thoughts of the last "bitter hour," to listen
to the "still voice" of nature. Having taken Bryant's advice, Whitman is meditating, at the outset of his poem, in the "still woods."
But rather than being reassured, Whitman is startled: what he

regarded as "safest," he now sees is composed of death, sickness, decay. Nature is nothing but "leavings":

> This is the compost of billions of premature corpses,
> Perhaps every mite has once formed part of a sick person.
>
> [*LG 1856*, p. 203]

In his desire to pierce to the meaning of nature, he contemplates reenacting the horrible violation of the "rude swain" of "Thanatopsis," who plows through and treads upon decaying bodies:

> I will run a furrow with my plough—I will press my spade
>   through the sod, and turn it up underneath,
> I am sure I shall expose some of the foul meat.
>
> [*LG 1856*, p. 203]

Bryant had imagined a rough farmer disturbing a grave, but Whitman heightens the drama by claiming that he personally will expose "foul meat."

Alan Trachtenberg has argued that Whitman, as the "poet of health," confirms himself "most reliably when confronting disease, decay, and death."[14] Whitman's affirmations gain strength from his hard-headed refusal to ignore destruction. The penultimate section of "This Compost" marvels at nature:

> What chemistry!
> That the winds are really not infectious!
> That this is no cheat, this transparent green-wash of the
>   sea, which is so amorous after me!
> That it is safe to allow it to lick my naked body all over with
>   its tongues!
> That it will not endanger me with the fevers that have
>   deposited themselves in it.
>
> [*LG 1856*, p. 204]

When he comes to realize that every spear of the grass he reclines on "rises out of what was once a catching disease," he exclaims: "Now I am terrified at the earth!" Whereas Bryant worked to achieve affirmation and calm in facing nature and death, Whitman acknowledges that he is disconcerted—nearly overwhelmed—by the transformative powers of nature. For Whitman, nature is "calm and patient" and thus alarmingly incomprehensible in its ability to grow "sweet things out of such corruptions," to distill "exquisite winds out of such infused fetor." Whitman's fear results as much from the mystery of the life force—from sex and the body—as it does from death. The poet finds the generation of loveliness out of leavings to be discomfiting and unfathomable.

The disastrous response to the 1856 edition—"Walt Whitman's greatest failure," according to Gay Wilson Allen—induced a process of change in the poet.[15] His book ignored by critics and buyers, Whitman sank into "an obstinate three year dumbness."[16] When he emerged in 1859 with "A Child's Reminiscence" (later, "Out of the Cradle Endlessly Rocking"), he appeared as a writer less opposed to literary conventions. His shift in style coincided with a new breakthrough in institutional acceptance: he placed the poem in the *Saturday Press*, a magazine nearly equal in prestige to the *Atlantic Monthly*.[17] In yet another anonymous review of his own work he compared the new poem with the two editions of *Leaves of Grass*, indicating that he still sought a broad reading public: "Those former issues, published by the author himself in little pittance-editions, on trial, have just dropped the book enough to ripple the inner first-circles of literary agitation, in immediate contact with it. The vast, extending, and ever-wider-extending circles, of the general supply, perusal, and discussion of such a work, have still to come. The market needs today to be supplied—the great West especially—with copious thousands of copies."[18] Neglect had not pushed Whitman into a desire to shun possible audiences. The dream was too compelling. Whitman lived with the hope that he could reach with one language both such intellectuals as Emerson, Thoreau, and Alcott and innumerable common laborers.

In 1859 Whitman made numerous adjustments to the "market [that] needs to-day to be supplied." In his anonymous review, he still described himself as the primitive rough, yet he also—and this was new—wanted people to note his "method" in "construction." Aware of earlier charges of formlessness, he now highlighted the issue of his artistry:

> Then the workmanship, the art-statement and argument of the question. Is this man really any artist at all? Or not plainly a sort of naked and hairy savage, come among us, with yelps and howls, disregarding all our lovely metrical laws? How can it be that he offends so many and so much? . . .
>
> Walt Whitman's method in the construction of his songs is strictly the method of Italian Opera, which, when heard, confounds the new person aforesaid, and, as far as he can then see, showing no purport for him, nor on the surface, nor any analogy to his previous-accustomed tunes, impresses him as if all the sounds of earth and hell were tumbled promiscuously together.[19]

Whitman rightly notes the importance of Italian opera to his poem. "Out of the Cradle" calls to mind the opera in numerous ways, including the mention of "aria" and "recitative," but the work was much more profoundly influenced by a series of English and American poems linking birds with poetic inspiration. Whitman's mention of the opera gets at the truth indirectly, however, in that it acknowledges the incorporation into his poetry of musical qualities associated with Tennyson and Poe.[20] "Out of the Cradle" is Whitman's crux poem, written when his powers were in an ideal balance, when he retained all the vitality of his early work and before the musicality of his later style had become too excessive, mannered, and inflated.

Both in structure and theme, "Out of the Cradle" illustrates that Whitman was consciously taking new directions. In this first of Whitman's poems based on a narrative structure, he recollects his childhood observation of two mockingbirds from Alabama. His own capacity for song is understood only after hearing the carol of love, longing, and grief produced by the he-bird calling to his lost mate. As several commentators have noted recently, this poem is linked to the "Calamus" sequence.[21] He is announcing, among other things, the centrality of his sexual identity to his creativity.

Yet with Whitman one bold step is usually countered by a cautious one. It is not accidental that the daring move is accompanied by a return to more traditional techniques. Whitman provides here a fundamentally different account of his poetic origins from anything found in the first two editions. Now he indicates that his inspiration comes not from journeys into the self, nor through an unmediated response to experience, but by "treasur-[ing] every note" of another singer, by "repeating" and "translating" and transmuting the song of a predecessor. As Stephen Whicher has argued, it is appropriate to attach a special meaning to Whitman's selection of "Out of the Cradle" as the first public evidence of his return to song. Whicher contends that "in this 'reminiscence' of the birth of his poetic vocation he is actually celebrating its recovery."[22] I would modify the argument, however, by suggesting that Whitman celebrates not merely the recovery but the very birth of his vocation, his birth as a significantly different kind of poet. He has been awakened by song, awakened by an *American* bird, with the result that "already a thousand singers—a thousand songs, clearer, louder, more sorrowful than yours, / A thousand warbling echoes have started to life within me." Longfellow, in *Evangeline*, praised the mockingbird as the "wildest of singers," and Thomas Jefferson declared that this bird made the English nightingale, in comparison, a "third-rate singer." As a New World bird and a mimic, the mockingbird is belated, but it is by no means silenced or subdued or diminished.

Whitman was quite accurate in calling "Out of the Cradle" an "art-statement," for, as Leo Spitzer has perceived, the poem is a "powerful synthesis of motifs" about birds that had developed over a period of fifteen hundred years in occidental poetry, ranging from the classical myth of Philomela to Whitman's own time.[23] The most important context of the poem is the work of Whitman's contemporaries and immediate predecessors in both England and America, who habitually linked the songs of birds and poets. "Out of the Cradle," in a way far more compelling than Whitman's revisions of "Thanatopsis," invites comparison with other poetry—specifically, Poe's "The Raven," Wordsworth's "To the Cuckoo" and "The Boy of Winander," Shelley's "To the Skylark," and Keats's "To a Nightingale."[24]

Whitman's engagement with Poe is more obvious but less telling than his transformation of the romantics. In "Out of the Cradle" he relies less on the solid, sensory description characteristic of the first two editions of *Leaves* (what the poet called words "as solid as timbers, stones, iron, brick, glass, planks, etc") than on a visionary vocabulary and ominous imagery to depict the interior landscape.[25] Whitman shows a new fondness for mood-impregnated, chiefly "nocturnal" imagery—the very imagery he occasionally objected to in Poe. He now uses such humanizing epithets and modifiers as "tender and pensive waves," "the mystic play of shadows twining and twisting as if they were alive," and "the yellow half-moon, late-risen, and swollen as if with tears." He apparently also learned from Poe how to use the striking musical device of the present participle in the medial and final positions to produce the effect of rhyming.[26] This device, used by Poe in "The Raven," appears in the famous strophe beginning "The aria sinking."

Some critics argue that Whitman unconsciously echoed "The Raven," but it seems more likely that he intended to benefit from Poe's notoriety.[27] It was Whitman's prerogative, of course, to allude to this poem, to adopt some of its successful techniques, and to create in his own poem a pattern resembling the symbols, diction, and episodes of "The Raven." Whitman recognized that "The Raven" was widely admired and enjoyed, and he himself saw strengths in it and recited it frequently.[28] Moreover, in 1857 Whitman the journalist quoted "The Raven" without attribution, confident that his readers would be familiar with the work.[29] In "Out of the Cradle," the most obvious echo of "The Raven" is the use of Poe's refrain "Nevermore":

> O throes!
> O you demon, singing by yourself—projecting me,
> O solitary me, listening—never more shall I cease
>   imitating, perpetuating you,
> Never more shall I escape,
> Never more shall the reverberations,
> Never more the cries of unsatisfied love be absent from me,
> Never again leave me to be the peaceful child I was before
>   what there, in the night,
> By the sea, under the yellow and sagging moon,
> The dusky demon aroused—the fire, the sweet hell within,
> The unknown want, the destiny of me.
>
> [*LG 1860*, p. 276]

In all likelihood Whitman sought direct comparison with Poe in "Out of the Cradle" so as to highlight his own projected image: his stress on healthiness and inspiration from nature as opposed to Poe's morbid and lore-inspired themes.

Whitman wanted to be compared with Poe, but "Out of the Cradle" is not marked by anxious competitiveness. The elaborate chain of transmission presented in the poem—from mockingbird to child, child to "fierce old mother" the sea, sea to bard—results in an echoing song that minimizes (at an overt level) the sense of intertextual struggle. The voices depend on each other.[30] Here Whitman presents himself as a vital link in the chain of transmission rather than as the maker of the chain itself.

The major romantic bird poems differ from "The Raven" in that we find, hovering behind them all, Ovid's *Metamorphoses* and the nightingale myth—the story of a woman who is raped, whose tongue is torn out so that she cannot tell her story, and who is then turned into a bird that can at least lament, though unintelligibly, her woes. As is common in Ovid, the tale concerns the loss of human voice and thus of the inability to express a great tragedy. Whereas in Ovid the movement is from the human to an inhuman and inarticulate world, the romantics typically move in the reverse direction by attempting to liberate nature's voice so that it becomes a power through the poet. This becomes clearest in Keats, who at times quite consciously inverts the Ovidian pattern by having natural objects awakened into speech (as, for example, when Lamia, a snake, becomes a woman). Still, Wordsworth, Shelley, and Keats talk about the bird's song without letting us hear it. What is particularly striking about Whitman's poem is that, while sustaining the traditional theme of loss, he renders the voice of the bird, giving us its song. Thus Whitman moves farther in the romantic reversal of the Ovidian pattern. He thereby makes a clear claim to being a greater poet of this world: he does not impose the human upon the natural, or merely describe the natural, but allows nature to speak through his poem.[31]

The paradox of "Out of the Cradle"—indeed one of the paradoxes of Whitman's entire career—is that he is an innovator, yet he is also the perpetuator of other works through his own. The old is present in the new; his highly distinctive poetry is molded from materials in the mainstream of literary tradition. "Out of the Cradle" is Whitman's virtuoso display of how rich a sense of tradition this supposed "rough" had, how completely wrong were those who took his pose literally, how many allusions he could pack into a poem, and how he could nonetheless make good his claim of being the poet closest to nature. As with "Pictures," to appreciate how various sources contributed to the poem is to understand a central theme of the work. In lines that close the first movement of "Out of the Cradle," Whitman clarified both his method and purpose in alluding to other poets:

> I, chanter of pains and joys, uniter of here and hereafter,
> Taking all hints to use them—but swiftly leaping beyond
>   them,
> A reminiscence sing.
>
> > [*LG 1860*, p. 270]

The presence of the past is most apparent in Whitman's works dealing with death. D. H. Lawrence expressed memorably what many readers have understood—that death pervades the poet's vision: "Walt's great poems are really huge fat tomb-plants, great rank graveyard growths."[32] The "grass over graves," as Lewis Hyde observes, comes to stand "for more than enduring life in Whitman's cosmology. It stands for the creative self, the singing self. Not only does the grass sprout from the grave, but it speaks; it is 'so many uttering tongues' emerging from 'the faint red roofs' of the mouths of the dead."[33] In the first three editions, Whitman's treatment of predecessors is marked by interconnections between life, death, and democracy. He commented in the

1855 Preface, "Past and present and future are not disjoined but joined. The greatest poet forms the consistence of what is to be from what has been and is. He drags the dead out of their coffins and stands them again on their feet . . . he says to the past, Rise and walk before me that I may realize you. He learns the lesson . . . he places himself where the future becomes present" (*LG 1855*, p. 12). By reinscribing elements of past works into a present poem, Whitman engages in an act of recovering and recording, of renewal and reinvigoration. His greatest successes rely on a delicate balance of old and new, established themes and devices in innovative forms and tones.

"So long!"—the poem that closes the 1860 edition—is a model of this method. In the late 1850s, Whitman began to consider writing a poem called "L'Envoy" (*NUPM* 4:1352). Whitman was thoroughly familiar with Longfellow's work and thus would have known his "L'Envoi," the conclusion and poetical summary of *Voices of the Night*. (That the tradition of "L'Envoi" poems goes back to Ovid and works its way up through the French Middle Ages and then to Chaucer and a host of English and American followers probably added to its fascination for Whitman.) Matters of crucial importance to Whitman were dealt with in Longfellow's poem:

> Ye voices, that arose
> After the Evening's close,
> And whispered to my restless heart repose!
>
> Go, breathe it in the ear
> Of all who doubt and fear,
> And say to them, "Be of good cheer!"
>
> . . . .
>
> Tongues of the dead, not lost,
> But speaking from death's frost,
> Like fiery tongues at Pentecost!

Glimmer, as funeral lamps,
Amid the chills and damps
Of the vast plain where Death encamps![34]

The subject matter—the connection between the tongues of the
dead, the voice of the poet, and the ear of the audience—was of
special importance to Whitman. Instead of producing his own
projected "L'Envoy," Whitman developed his brilliant vernacular
transformation of the tradition, "So long!" This poem is represen-
tative of early Whitman in that its sources are so hidden as to be
only barely discernible. Although it draws on literary sources (including Whitman's own previous work, for example, in the reference to "electric"), the poem finally insists on denying its literary
qualities. Whitman explained to William Sloane Kennedy that the
expression "So long!" was a "salutation of departure, greatly
used among sailors, sports, and prostitutes. The sense of it is 'Till
we meet again,'—conveying an inference that somehow they will
doubtless so meet, sooner or later" (*CRE*, p. 503 *n*). Whitman's
"So long!" is a sign of parting and of departing from literary tradition. Most "L'Envoi" poems call attention to their own fictive
quality. Whitman reverses this pattern by denying his literariness:
"This is no book, / Who touches this touches a man" (*LG 1860*,
p. 455).

In his greatest phase, the years 1855 to 1860, Whitman is
interested in the nick of time where two eternities, past and future, meet in the present. At the "flexible doors," at the entrance
to the grave and the exit from the womb, at the shore's edge: he
situates himself repeatedly at thresholds. His treatment of his
central image, leaves of grass, illustrates his complex sense of
time. Thus, in "So long!" Whitman claimed: "All I have done, I
would cheerfully give to be trod under foot, if it might only be the
soil of superior poems" (*LG 1860*, p. 452). Like leaves of grass
themselves, poems rise again and again out of decaying remains.

 CHAPTER FOUR

Crisis and Control in
the Late Phase

Whitman revised his work more radically than any other American poet before or since. As early as 1865, while retaining his long free-verse line, he turned increasingly to inversions, literary diction, and other poeticisms.[1] He turned also to a more overtly allusive style, signaling a renegotiation of his relationship with other poets.

Crises may account for Whitman's extreme self-revision: national fragmentation in war was followed by the personal traumas of the Harlan debacle (whereby he lost his government job because of the supposed "immorality" of *Leaves of Grass*) and of his declining health, leading to a paralytic stroke. Forces of destruction and disorder stimulated his desire to be a joiner and a healer, to find a more soothing voice, to establish a tone of cultural maturity. In a way that parallels the career development of his major English counterparts, Browning, Arnold, and Tennyson, Whitman hoped to make certain concessions to literary fashion without compromising the perceptions central to his original creative impulse.[2]

Yet most modern readers do find him compromised. Lack of energy, failure of vision, quirk of temperament—for some reason Whitman fell into a gentility contrary to his nature. Only rarely in the postwar years did he write with the power and complexity of the early poetry. His best late work appears when he undertakes a life review, most notably in "When Lilacs Last in the Dooryard Bloom'd" (1865) and *Specimen Days* (1882).[3]

The Postwar Poetry in Context

Following the disruption of the Civil War and a booming economic expansion, many American authors sensed a need for a stable, ordered art. In *Parnassus*, a compendium produced by Emerson and his daughter Edith, the Concord sage stressed "the necessity of printing in every collection many masterpieces which all English-speaking men have agreed in admiring," a necessity all the more acute in convulsive times.[4] The New England poets, with their translations, worked to preserve the European literary tradition (Longfellow translated the *Divine Comedy*, Bryant the *Iliad* and *Odyssey*, Emerson the *Vita Nuova*). Whitman, too, became less experimental, echoing repeatedly nineteenth-century favorites, Longfellow and Tennyson—poets who were themselves echo chambers of earlier poetry.

It is clear that the late Whitman meant to function as an unofficial poet laureate. Lacking an aristocratic system of patronage, the laureate in a democracy, he concluded, required other kinds of validation (from influential critics and reviewers, from publishers, from sales). The broad cultural endorsement of Longfellow helps explain why Whitman repeatedly invoked him in the late poetry. When Whitman read "Thou Mother with Thy Equal Brood" at Dartmouth College in 1872, he took his cue from Longfellow's poem "The Building of the Ship." Whitman's attention had been drawn to Longfellow's peroration:

> Thou, too, sail on, O Ship of State!
> Sail on, o UNION, strong and great!
> Humanity with all its fears,
> With all the hopes of future years
> Is hanging breathless on thy fate!

Whitman himself eventually rode this ship, as one sees in "Thou Mother with Thy Equal Brood":

> Sail, sail thy best, ship of Democracy,
> Of value is thy freight, 'tis not the Present only,
> The Past is also stored in thee,
> Thou holdest not the venture of thyself alone, not of the
>   Western continent alone,
> Earth's *résumé* entire floats on thy keel O Ship, is steadied
>   by thy spars.[5]

Whitman's passage, when taken in isolation, has seemed "trite" to modern readers; when placed next to its source it seems doubly so.[6]

At times, Whitman was even more obvious in urging readers to think about *Leaves* and Longfellow at once. He appropriated titles from Longfellow, as when he named one group of his own poems "Birds of Passage" (*CRE,* pp. 226–41). Moreover, a work first appearing in the 1856 *Leaves* as "Poem of the Heart of the Son of Manhattan Island" in 1867 became "Excelsior." Given the extraordinary fame of Longfellow's 1841 "Excelsior," this renaming could not have been coincidental. The "Blue Book" *Leaves* (his annotated copy of the 1860 edition) shows that he twice crossed out "Excelsior" as a title only to settle on it a final, third time.[7] The change in title points to a transformed meaning and an inner struggle over time. In the earliest version of the poem, with its unvarying pattern of questions, he ironically comments on the refrain of Longfellow's youthful hero who, striving ever upward, chants "excelsior." Longfellow's hero was endlessly aspiring, but his quest resulted in defeat and death. In contrast, Whitman begins his poem with confidence: "Who has gone farthest? For I swear I will go farther" (LG 1856, p. 255). He also compares himself with other poets, including Longfellow, declaring "And who has projected beautiful words through the longest time? By God! I will outvie him! I will say such words, they shall stretch through longer time" (LG 1856, p. 256). Yet this line was expunged in 1881, when Whitman sought reconciliation with other American poets. What began as a poem unflattering to Longfellow ultimately became a tribute to him. In borrowing the "Excelsior" title Whitman was not wresting credit from Longfellow but directing readers to consider his work both against and within the sphere of high culture.

One critic notes that in the 1860s Whitman becomes "blatantly conventional, and often he imitates other poets, as if seeking inspiration from the popular appeal of their verse."[8] (The "as if" testifies to the reluctance of critics to believe that a major artist might seek inspiration from public art.) Tired of charges that his work lacked artistry and anxious to assume the role of public poet, Whitman attempted to enrich his verse by incorporating other voices without abandoning his own distinctive sound and manner. Too often, however, Whitman lost sight of his own oppositional purpose in his bid for acclaim. In "Pioneers! O Pioneers!" (1865), for example, the sentiment, diction, and meter sound more like Longfellow than like Whitman, who clearly wrote this poem with the pounding rhythms of "Hiawatha" in mind.

A similar movement from a dismissive to a respectful attitude is seen in Whitman's changing stance toward Tennyson. He did nothing to resist William Douglas O'Connor's transformation of his own image from the "rough" into the "good gray poet," the latter tag inspired by a line in Tennyson's "Ode on the Death of Wellington."⁹ Moreover, he was elated that Tennyson "discovered great 'go'" in *Leaves*, asserting that this was a "big certificate" as important as Emerson's famous letter of 1855 (*C* 2:126; *NUPM* 3:1231). Whitman's respect for Tennyson appears in his assertion in "Song of the Exposition" that European culture was "Blazon'd with Shakespeare's purple page / And dirged by Tennyson's sweet sad rhyme" (*CRE*, p. 198). Yet for all his merit, Whitman believed that Tennyson could not overcome his role as spokesman for a declining culture.

This view of Tennyson's cultural role shapes Whitman's most important poem indebted to the English laureate. On a clipping that provided subject matter for "Prayer of Columbus" (1874), Whitman noted: "read first *Ulysses* by Tennyson."¹⁰ Whitman was now content to imitate the mood, setting, tone, and form of Tennyson's poem. As in "Ulysses," the speaker voices a fatigued but impassioned readiness for experience. "Prayer of Columbus" embodies the theme of Europe coming to America and highlights the transformation of the old when it contacts the new. The meeting of past and present, of old ways and new circumstances, yields "newer, better worlds." Despite the borrowings from "Ulysses," Whitman establishes his work as more oriented to the future than Tennyson's. Unlike Ulysses, who seeks to repeat past triumphs, Whitman's Columbus yearns for change and a time when his discoveries will be celebrated. The "anthems in new tongues" saluting Columbus hail and revere him. In Columbus's ultimate vindication, Whitman finds hope that future poets will endorse and justify *Leaves of Grass*.

"Prayer" has been faulted on the grounds that it is not Columbus's meditation but Whitman's prayer about Whitman and thus undermined by sentimental self-pity.¹¹ Yet Whitman was striving to write not a dramatic monologue in the manner of

Browning's "My Last Duchess" or "Andrea del Sarto" but a mask lyric like "Ulysses." In a helpful essay, Ralph Rader distinguishes between poems in which we regard the speaker as clearly "other" than the author and those in which the speaker is a mask through which the poet speaks.[12] In creating Ulysses and Columbus, Tennyson and Whitman produce outward correlatives of emotions experienced by the poets themselves. We are meant to feel the poets in these works. (Tennyson remarked that, better than anything in *In Memoriam*, "Ulysses" expressed his need for continuing after the death of Hallam. And Anne Gilchrist pointed out what Whitman himself acknowledged to be an "autobiographical dash" in "Prayer.")[13] Instead of seeing the failure to produce Columbus's prayer as an indulgence in sentimentality, it is more accurate to see Whitman—in one of the bleakest years of his life, the year following his stroke and the death of his mother—projecting his emotions onto a mask figure as a technique to control and objectify emotions and events that threatened to overwhelm him.

The talent that was so remarkable in the early Whitman—the ability to absorb fully the work of others and turn it to his ends— seems to have drained away from the poet. In fact, he impoverishes rather than enriches his voice whenever he echoes too closely Longfellow and Tennyson, those poets who had achieved both popular and critical success. Whitman's own bid for comparable success, by creating a discrepancy between critical attitude and poetic means, led to a hollowness in much of his postwar poetry. As *Specimen Days* reveals, Whitman still held tough-minded critical opinions that hampered the "good gray poet" (see figure 2) from successfully making poetic gestures he could not fully believe in.

"When Lilacs Last in the Dooryard Bloom'd" shows what the late style might have been. Reminiscent of "Out of the Cradle" in

Figure 2. Photograph of Whitman by Alexander Gardner, ca. 1864. Courtesy of Walt Whitman Collection (NY5-1656-G), Clifton Waller Barrett Library, Manuscripts Division, University of Virginia Library.

its formal qualities, "Lilacs" possesses a rich allusiveness, making it more complex than other postwar poems. Here Whitman's allusiveness is thoroughly sincere. As with "Out of the Cradle," the subject of death prompts a more ritualized poetry and a concern with tradition, but now he moves away from a private consideration of death to a public figure and a public poetry. In "Lilacs," Whitman draws on pastoral elegy, one of the highest and oldest literary traditions in western culture. He employs many conventions of pastoral elegy, notably the funeral procession, the mourning of nature with pathetic fallacy, the bestowing of flowers on the coffin, and the contrast between nature's renewal and the interruption of death.[14] The many elegiac elements make his departures from the form stand out. Most significantly, Whitman refuses—despite his apostrophes to star, bird, lilacs, and death—to address Lincoln. (Whitman eliminates the singular person by enlarging his subject: "Nor for you, for one alone. . . .") The president can never again be addressed in person, and by abandoning the address to him, Whitman insists on the value of truth, stark and painful though it may be.

Whitman de-Christianizes the form through recourse to Greek mythology and Egyptian burial customs and by avoiding the usual apotheosis. The allusion to the Egyptian practice of adorning the tombs of pharaohs with hieroglyphics emphasizes the democratic nature of the poem: the pictures Whitman hangs on the tomb are of a largely agrarian American republic. In pastoral elegies, the person mourned is often depicted as a poet and the mourner as his successor, but in Whitman's democratic elegy, the key figure is a leader and a "comrade."

The assassination of Lincoln, Whitman's political alter ego, threw both national politics and Whitman's poetics into a moment of crisis that prompted him to undertake a life review, to turn back on his own history and on the history of his poetic compositions.

With fine insight, Helen Vendler has explored Whitman's echoing
of many of his earlier poems, notably "Out of the Cradle," "There
Was a Child Went Forth," and "Pictures."[15] Lincoln's death also
turned Whitman's attention back to his earlier poem "To Think of
Time," which took on new edge.

> Slowmoving and black lines creep over the whole
>   earth . . . . they never cease . . . . they are the burial
>   lines,
> He that was President was buried, and he that is now
>   President shall surely be buried.
>
> [*LG 1855*, p. 99]

The black lines described in 1855 seemed to Whitman to be spread-
ing across the New York sky ten years later on the day of the
president's death (April 15, 1865): "black, black, black—as you
look toward the sky—long broad black like great serpents slowly
undulating in every direction."[16] "Lilacs" traces Lincoln's own
"long and winding" burial procession and in so doing reconsiders
"To Think of Time," a work that, under different circumstances,
overcame the fear of death's "earth-beetles" and the horror that
all things might come to "ashes of dung" with the assertion: "I
swear I think there is nothing but immortality!" In "Lilacs" Whitman confronts the "debris and debris of all dead soldiers" and
resists even his own affirmations of faith in immortality. Nor does
he take comfort, as he had earlier in his career, in the idea that an
individual is one particle of the universal life and that death leads
to endless regeneration of new life. Having witnessed amputa-
tions, gangrene, and piled limbs outside of Civil War hospitals,
Whitman seeks release and praises death as the "strong deliv-
eress." When life appears purposeless and profane, death looks
"sane and sacred."

In "Lilacs" Whitman offers the perceptions of a poet chastened by war and assassination. Whitman's echoing of himself represents a concerted effort to create a new, muted, less celebratory vision, consciously nonoptimistic. With regard to poetic predecessors, he does more than establish a middle position between boastful independence and slavish reliance. He enlarges his undertaking by making the techniques of others—including his earlier self—work for present needs and his own voice.

Whitman on Other Writers: Controlled "Graciousness" in Specimen Days

In the postwar period Whitman found himself in an odd position, for just as he moved, in his poetry, toward acceptance of competitors he was met by a curious practice of exclusion. Anthologies compiled in the 1870s by Emerson, Bryant, and Whittier helped solidify a newly emerging canon. These poet-anthologists all assumed that there existed distinct groups of major and minor American poets. The major poets, they decided, were themselves, Holmes, Longfellow, and Lowell. They ranked Poe as a minor figure, and all excluded Whitman.[17] The author of *Leaves* responded with an anonymous blast in the *West Jersey Press:* "Will it not prove a pretty page of the history of our literature a couple of decades hence, that in 1874–5 Emerson, Bryant and Whittier each made great Omnibus-gatherings of all the current poets and poetry—putting in such as Nora Perry and Charles Gayler and carefully leaving Walt Whitman out?"[18]

Bitterness stemming from exclusion helps explain Whitman's purpose in undertaking, in 1880, the "ungracious task" of describing the shortcomings of Ralph Waldo Emerson.[19] Whitman wrote "Emerson's Books" for the May 22, 1880, issue of *The Literary World*, which was, essentially, a festschrift for Emerson's seventy-seventh birthday. All the other contributions lauded and sanctified the Sage of Concord. Only Whitman dared fault the Master.[20] Deliberately directing his attention toward the "bare spots and darknesses" rather than the "sunny expanses" of Emerson's work, Whitman wonders "if Emerson really knows or feels what Poetry is at its highest." He explains that of "*power* [Emerson] seems to have a gentleman's admiration—but in his inmost heart the grandest attribute of God and Poets is always subordinate to the octaves, conceits, polite kinks, and verbs" (*PW* 2:517). He further complains that Emerson's art is not organic: "It is always a *make*, never an unconscious *growth*." Although the Concord poet speaks eloquently of nature, his productions are merely the "porcelain figure or statuette of lion, or stag, or Indian hunter . . . never the animal itself, or the hunter himself" (*PW* 2:515). Finally, Whitman makes a clear and careful effort to detach himself from a former influence. Emersonianism becomes something notably limited, something one passes beyond: "The reminiscence that years ago I began like most youngsters to have a touch (though it came late, and was only on the surface) of Emerson-on-the-brain—that I read his writings reverently, and address'd him in print as 'Master,' and for a month or so thought of him as such—I retain not only with composure, but positive satisfaction. I have noticed that most young people of eager minds pass through this stage of exercise" (*PW* 2:517).

Against these specific criticisms—and against Whitman's larger claim in "Democratic Vistas" that American poets produced only "perpetual, pistareen, paste-pot work"—stands Whitman's conciliatory *Specimen Days*, in which he praises Poe and Carlyle and devotes an entire chapter, "My Tribute to Four Poets," to commending a "mighty four" of American poetry: Longfellow, Bryant, Whittier, and Emerson heading the list.[21] An examination of the carefully controlled graciousness of *Specimen*

Days reveals much about the role the aging Whitman assumed for himself in American poetry.

One of Whitman's reasons for ranking Emerson highest among American poets only a year after detailing his great faults can be found within the "Tribute."[22] Whitman remarks that a reviewer "who ought to know better, speaks of my 'attitude of contempt and scorn and intolerance' toward the leading poets— of my 'deriding' them, and preaching their 'uselessness'" (*PW* 1:266). The reviewer is Edmund Clarence Stedman, whose "Walt Whitman" in the November 1880 issue of *Scribner's Monthly*, though generally laudatory, criticizes Whitman's attitude toward his fellow poets:

> The "Leaves of Grass," in thought and method, avowedly are a protest against a hackney breed of singers, singing the same old song. More poets than one are born in each generation, yet Whitman has derided his compeers, scouted the sincerity of their passion, and has borne on his mouth Heine's sneer at the eunuchs singing of love.
>
> Doubtless his intolerant strictures upon the poets of his own land and time have made them hesitate to venture upon the first advances in brotherhood, or to intrude on him with their recognition of his birthright. . . . [H]is opinion of their uselessness has been expressed in withering terms.

Though he concedes that the quality of much American poetry leaves room for complaint, Stedman recommends a larger view: "I should not be writing this series of papers, did I not well know that there are other poets than himself who hear the roll of the ages, who look before and after, above and below."[23]

After the severe judgments handed down in "Democratic Vistas" and "Emerson's Books," one wonders why Whitman

thought Stedman "ought to know better." Throughout his poetic
career until the "Tribute," Whitman had never praised American
poets as a group except in one brief, little-publicized interview.[24]
Curiously, even in the postwar years, when Whitman's poetry
began to include friendly allusions to such writers as Longfellow,
he had continued to belittle his fellow poets in essays and interviews. Stedman's remarks cut Whitman deeply because they
made him sensitive to the discrepancy that had developed between his critical remarks and his poetry. In *Specimen Days* Whitman responds to Stedman's charges by offering gentle, vague
approval based upon a sense of placement and history. Whitman
concluded that a generous acceptance of other poets would en-
hance his own image as the national bard. With the more important image of himself as a creator of "dislocating agitation and
shock" firmly established, the time had come to be gracious.[25]

Although Whitman is all-embracing in his "Tribute," there
are signs of restraint:

> A short but pleasant visit to Longfellow. I am not one of
> the calling kind, but as the author of "Evangeline" kindly
> took the trouble to come and see me three years ago in
> Camden, where I was ill, I felt not only the impulse of my own
> pleasure on that occasion, but a duty. . . .
>
> And now just here I feel the impulse to interpolate some-
> thing about the mighty four who stamp this first American
> century with its birthmarks of poetic literature. . . . I can't
> imagine any better luck befalling these States for a poetical
> beginning and initiation than has come from Emerson, Long-
> fellow, Bryant, and Whittier. Emerson, to me, stands un-
> mistakably at the head, but for the others I am at a loss where
> to give any precedence. Each illustrious, each rounded, each
> distinctive. Emerson for his sweet, vital-tasting melody,
> rhym'd philosophy, and poems as amber-clear as the honey

of the wild bee he loves to sing. Longfellow for rich color, graceful forms and incidents—all that makes life beautiful and love refined—competing with the singers of Europe on their own ground, and, with one exception, better and finer work than that of any of them. Bryant pulsing the first interior verse-throbs of a mighty world—bard of the river and the wood, ever conveying a taste of open air, with scents as from hayfields, grapes, birch-borders—always lurkingly fond of threnodies—beginning and ending his long career with chants of death, with here and there through all . . . touching the highest universal truths, enthusiasms, duties—morals as grim and eternal, if not as stormy and fateful, as anything in Eschylus. While in Whittier, with his special themes—(his outcropping love of heroism and war, for all his Quakerdom, his verses at times like the measur'd step of Cromwell's old veterans)—in Whittier lives the zeal, the moral energy, that founded New England—the splendid rectitude and ardor of Luther, Milton, George Fox—I must not, dare not, say the wilfulness and narrowness—though doubtless the world needs now, and always will need, almost above all, just such narrowness and wilfulness. [*PW* 1:266–67]

Whitman's account of his visit to Longfellow qualifies the "Tribute" by placing it in the realm of social courtesy; he is dutifully paying his respects in a context where harsh criticism would be inappropriate. Though he conforms to the manners of society, this conformity does not threaten his separate integrity: Whitman remains a man of independent thought here, "not one of the calling kind." Tolerant in his judgments, he carefully limits praise. Words like "birthmarks," "beginning," "initiation" indicate that these poets are the first exponents of a growing tradition rather than a culmination within it. In spite of an allusion to Emerson's superiority and in spite of more wholehearted praise of Emerson and Bryant, Whitman's use of parataxis in the passage suggests a rough equality among his subjects—an equality that implies reserved judgment.[26] Similar reservations are evident in Whitman's praise of the other writers in *Specimen Days*, Carlyle and Poe. A look at Whitman's handling of these six writers, from the highest to the lowest, reveals an interesting approach to conciliation.

The brief statement on Emerson in the "Tribute" does not fully explain the reason for his being "at the head," although the references to the "vital-tasting melody" and "wild bee" seem to praise the freedom of Emerson's lines. In noting that the poems are "as amber-clear as the honey of the wild bee he loves to sing," Whitman implicitly applauds Emerson's concrete use of nature.[27] And the mention of "rhym'd philosophy" emphasizes the importance of thought in Emerson's meter-making arguments. These brief remarks identify—they do not evaluate—the salient features of Emerson's work.

A subsequent chapter, "By Emerson's Grave," is more expansive and sheds additional light on Whitman's evaluation of Emerson. Whitman notes that

> the life now rounded and completed in its mortal development, and which nothing can change or harm more, has its most illustrious halo, not in its splendid intellectual or esthetic products, but as forming in its entirety one of the few, (alas! how few!) perfect and flawless excuses for being, of the entire literary class.
>
> We can say, as Abraham Lincoln at Gettysburg, It is not we who come to consecrate the dead—we reverently come to receive, if so it may be, some consecration to ourselves and daily work from him. [*PW* 1:290–91]

Although attention is given to Emerson's life rather than his writing, the tone and religious language of this passage indicate that Whitman's praise is more heartfelt here than in the "Tribute."[28]

Emerson's death has advanced the mollifying process Stedman's criticism had begun. (Later, death possibly softens Whitman's judgment of Bryant and almost certainly his assessments of Longfellow, Carlyle, and Poe.) A twilight air pervades *Specimen Days*, a feeling that all will be resolved with the coming of death. While alive, Emerson was a literary rival whom many considered the presiding master; thus, in "Emerson's Books," Whitman struggled to distance himself from his former mentor. But with Emerson's death, critical distance must have seemed a disadvantage. Now Whitman partakes of the holiness of the Concord sage, joining those who "reverently come to receive . . . some consecration to ourselves and daily work from him."

As Whitman applauds Emerson for his concrete use of nature, so he admires Bryant for the "taste of open air, with scents as from hayfields, grapes, birch-borders" in his verse. Bryant's use of the local scene gives him a distinctively native quality that makes him the first truly American poet, "pulsing the first interior verse-throbs of a mighty world." The chapter "Death of William Cullen Bryant" again stresses Bryant's role as a nature poet: he "loved Nature so fondly, and sung so well her shows and seasons" (*PW* 1:166). But as this is the only comment on Bryant's literary work in the entire chapter, Whitman may be suggesting a negative judgment by omission.

The "Tribute" praises, along with the nature themes, Bryant's concern with death—he is "lurkingly fond of threnodies." In 1871, in "Democratic Vistas," Whitman implied that America had few great poems on death: "In the future of these States must arise poets immenser far, and make great poems of death" (*PW* 2:420). Although all of Bryant's best poetry, including "Thanatopsis," was written well before 1840, he apparently was not "immense" enough for Whitman in the seventies.[29] But in 1882, *Specimen Days* finds him a poet of increased magnitude. Again, it is possible that Bryant's intervening death may have influenced Whitman, for now Bryant's work touches "universal truths" and contains "morals as grim and eternal . . . as anything in Eschylus," a comparison which elevates Bryant to impressive stature.

Whitman is more reserved, even ambivalent, about Longfellow. His praise is lavish, but his qualifications are devastating. The "Tribute" limits Longfellow's significance as a poet for "this first American century" by noting that with "one exception" he successfully competes "with the singers of Europe on their own ground." (The "one exception" is of course Tennyson who, in an aside, gets some of the highest praise bestowed in the "Tribute.") A subsequent chapter, "Death of Longfellow," describes Longfellow as "eminent" in the style and forms of poetical expression. But even the rites of death do not keep Whitman from noting "an idiosyncrasy, almost a sickness, of verbal melody" and from remarking that Longfellow is the "universal poet of women and young people" (*PW* 1:284–85).

Despite Longfellow's limitations, Whitman applauds him for including serious themes in his poetry. Death—as with Bryant—is one of his major concerns. But the author of *Evangeline* has a way of treating even this topic with "no undue element of pensiveness"; he strictly avoids "exceptional passions" (*PW* 1:285). Whitman notes that Longfellow is a soothing rather than a revolutionary poet, presenting "nothing offensive or new" in his work. As such, Longfellow has gained great popularity—but at the sacrifice of originality. Even when Whitman defends Longfellow's verse from the charge that it lacks "racy nativity and special originality," he does not deny the charge itself. Rather, he grants the point but adds that "ere the New World can be worthily original, and announce herself and her own heroes, she must be well saturated with the originality of others, and respectfully consider the heroes that lived before Agamemnon" (PW 1:286).

To gauge the comments on Longfellow, one must understand the great importance Whitman attached to originality. Whitman's own poetic practice was an attempt to fulfill the American poet's highest duty: to create "national, original archetypes in literature" (PW 2:405). Eleven years after this statement from "Democratic Vistas," he still stressed the importance of "national" originality; *Specimen Days* calls on poets to give up European models in favor of the American landscape—the "prairies, the Rocky mountains . . . the Mississippi and Missouri rivers" (PW 1:223). Nonetheless, though both works call for originality tied to a sense of the nation, *Specimen Days* reveals that Whitman has mellowed: genteel poets who follow European patterns are no longer necessarily producers of "pistareen, paste-pot work." Hence, in "Death of Longfellow" Whitman argues that Longfellow's polished lyrics are the sort of "counteractant most needed for our materialistic, self-assertive, money-worshipping . . . present age in America" (PW 1:285).

If Whitman qualified his complimentary remarks about Longfellow, his reservations about Whittier go beyond mere circumscription to the verge of outright attack. His focus is on the moral quality of the man. He compliments Whittier for having the "splendid rectitude and ardor" of a religious reformer, but he also quickly mentions less desirable qualities: "I must not, dare not, say the wilfulness and narrowness." Despite the disclaimer, the blow is delivered. Whitman finds in Whittier the Quaker both the strengths and the weaknesses of New England Calvinism.[30] The suggestion that "in Whittier lives the zeal, the moral energy, that founded New England" carries the New Yorker's regional suspicions.

Ambiguity marks the description of Whittier's "outcropping love of heroism and war, for all his Quakerdom, his verses at times like the measur'd step of Cromwell's old veterans." Whitman perceives the anomaly of a Quaker poet singing of war without disapproving of Whittier's use of this subject matter.[31] Yet the imagery conveys Whitman's ambivalent feelings: Cromwell might be admired by Americans for his Calvinist convictions and anti-monarchical stands, but he is nonetheless notable neither for compassion nor for love of art. Verse that steps like Cromwell and his old veterans, for all its manliness and vigor, is probably ponderous. To Whitman's way of thinking, these are rhythms reminiscent of the Old World—not native rhythms appropriate to New World heroes.[32]

In *Specimen Days*, Whitman also records mixed reactions to two other writers, Carlyle and Poe. Not surprisingly, Carlyle is held in higher regard than Poe. The Scotsman was an important influence whose enormous power and catalytic energy Whitman recognizes: without Carlyle, mid-nineteenth-century British literature would be "an army with no artillery" (*PW* 1:251). Still, Whitman quarrels with the uses Carlyle made of the power at his command; the artillery is not properly directed and thus gives rise to the central irony of Carlyle's life—he announces the malady of the age while being "himself . . . a mark'd illustration of it" (*PW* 1:261).

Although he does not have the proper answers, Carlyle nevertheless has merit. Unlike Longfellow, whose beautiful verse was a quiet rebuke to the materialism of the age, Carlyle violently hacks at the "jungle and poison-vines and underbrush" of the times (*PW* 1:255). Earlier in his career, however, Whitman saw Carlyle's rhetoric as more threatening. In fact, "Democratic Vistas" was written partly as a response to "Shooting Niagara" (*PW* 2:375–76). At the time of Whitman's 1871 essay, he thought Carlyle offered "the highest feudal point of view" and presented formidable arguments against the political theory of democracy. That Whitman is conciliatory in *Specimen Days* may be ascribed not only to Carlyle's death (see the chapter "Death of Thomas Carlyle") but also to Whitman's ability to bring Carlyle's thought more into accord with his own.[33] Although in *Specimen Days* he still must admit that Carlyle is no democrat, Whitman has come to think that the Scotsman provides "the most indignant . . . protest anent the fruits of feudalism to-day in Great Britain" (*PW* 1:251).

It is likely, also, that Whitman comes to terms with Carlyle because he sees the similarities between Carlyle's religious-poetic acts of prophecy and his own poetic creations. Whitman is truly fascinated with Carlyle the prophet. He even takes pains to explain that the word *prophecy* is "much misused; it seems narrow'd to prediction merely. That is not the main sense of the Hebrew word translated 'prophet;' it means one whose mind bubbles up and pours forth as a fountain, from inner, divine spontaneities revealing God. Prediction is a very minor part of prophecy. The great matter is to reveal and outpour the God-like suggestions pressing for birth in the soul" (*PW* 1:250). Whitman then points out that this is also "the doctrine of the Friends or Quakers." Because Whitman noted his own links with Quakerism in the opening chapters, and because so much of his poetry praises spontaneity, it is not surprising that Whitman, even with his songs of democracy, is willing to make allowances for Carlyle.

Real reconciliation, however, is blocked by the Scotsman's philosophical bleakness, an outlook that posed a growing threat to the aging and ailing American poet. Whitman, as the poet of the body, traces Carlyle's pessimism back to the body, back to his dyspepsia. He had "the best equipt, keenest mind . . . of all Britain; only he had an ailing body. Dyspepsia is to be traced in every page, and now and then fills the page. One may include among the lessons of his life . . . how behind the tally of genius and morals stands the stomach, and gives a sort of casting vote" (*PW* 1:249). Carlyle's bodily problems prevent him from being a complete and balanced man with "soul-sight."

> There is, apart from mere intellect, in the make-up of every superior human identity, (in its moral completeness, considered as *ensemble*, not for that moral alone, but for the whole being, including physique,) a wondrous something that realizes without argument, frequently without what is called education . . . an intuition of the absolute balance, in time and space, of the . . . general unsettledness, we call *the world*; a soul-sight of that divine clue and unseen thread which holds the whole congeries of things, all history and time, and all events . . . like a leash'd dog in the hand of the hunter. Such soul-sight and root-centre for the mind—mere optimism explains only the surface or fringe of it—Carlyle was mostly, perhaps entirely without. [*PW* 1:257-58]

He who believes most fully in the moral unity and sanity of the world has this "soul-sight" and is "the truest cosmical devotee or religioso." In contrast, he who sees darkness and despair in the workings of God's providence is "the most radical sinner and infidel" (*PW* 1:260). On this point Whitman cannot compromise. He was able to accept Carlyle's politics when he thought of his views as a protest against feudalism rather than the voice of feudalism, but no toying with perspective can correct Carlyle's dark outlook. What is interesting here is the extent to which Whitman does try to handle disagreement positively in *Specimen Days*. The above passage holds clues to the crucial importance of an encompassing strategy. Words like "completeness," "ensemble," "whole being," "absolute balance," and "the whole congeries of things" point to a larger need for harmony, place, and decorum. The tensions beneath this "wondrous something" are barely controlled in Whitman's final image. When all history becomes "a leash'd dog in the hand of the hunter," the balance strains and a ferocity beneath decorum reveals the effort, and hence the importance, of Whitman's benign mask.

Whitman's all-encompassing strategy comes under even greater tension when he discusses Poe. Poe is certainly at the bottom of the list of writers considered in *Specimen Days*, and it is no accident that he is not included among the eulogized group in "My Tribute to Four Poets." By 1881, Whitman thinks the nineteenth century is sick and that Poe is a mark of the malady. Poetry like Poe's—stressing the lush and the weird, morbidity and abnormal beauty—has taken "extraordinary possession of Nineteenth century verse-lovers" (*PW* 1:232). His poetry is "the abnegation of the perennial and democratic concretes at first hand, the body, the earth and sea, sex and the like—and the substitution of something for them at second or third hand." No verse could be farther from what Whitman wants. As he notes in the final sentence of *Specimen Days*, "the efforts of the true poets, founders, religions, literatures, all ages, have been . . . essentially the same—to bring people back from their persistent strayings and sickly abstractions, to the costless average, divine, original concrete" (*PW* 1:295).

But "Edgar Poe's Significance" contains other, more favorable statements on Poe. This chapter has two perspectives, that of 1875 and that of 1882. In the report reprinted from the Washington *Star* for November 18, 1875, at the time of the public reburial of Poe's remains, Whitman states that Poe has earned a "special recognition." Whitman's criticism in the report, though less cutting than the rest of the chapter, still carries an edge beyond the pleasant, socially acceptable comments one might expect on such an occasion:

"'For a long while, and until lately, I had a distaste for Poe's writings. I wanted, and still want for poetry, the clear sun shining, and fresh air blowing—the strength and power of health, not of delirium, even amid the stormiest passions—with always the background of the eternal moralities. Noncomplying with these requirements, Poe's genius has yet conquer'd a special recognition for itself, and I too have come to fully admit it, and appreciate it and him.

"'In a dream I once had, I saw a vessel on the sea, at midnight, in a storm. It was no great full-rigg'd ship, nor majestic steamer, steering firmly through the gale, but seem'd one of those superb little schooner yachts I had often seen lying anchor'd, rocking so jauntily, in the waters around New York, or up Long Island sound—now flying uncontroll'd with torn sails and broken spars through the wild sleet and winds and waves of the night. On the deck was a slender, slight, beautiful figure, a dim man, apparently enjoying all the terror, the murk, and the dislocation of which he was the centre and the victim. That figure of my lurid dream might stand for Edgar Poe, his spirit, his fortunes, and his poems—themselves all lurid dreams.'" [*PW* 1:232]

Whitman depicts himself as Poe's opposite: instead of murk, delirium, and a ship out of control, Whitman seeks sunshine, health, and a stable "background of the eternal moralities." Yet Whitman *was* there at the ceremony (the only major American writer in attendance), applauding Poe's special "genius."

In the essay framing the 1875 report, Whitman recognizes Poe's great poetic failings: his love of abstract beauty, his overindulgence in the "rhyming art," and his "incorrigible propensity toward nocturnal themes." Poe is one of the "electric lights of imaginative literature, brilliant and dazzling, but with no heat"—not a totally negative judgment in view of what the metaphor meant to the poet of "I Sing the Body Electric." In the end, he grants Poe a strange sort of usefulness: "there is nothing better . . . than a perfect and noble life, morally without flaw, happily balanced in activity, physically sound and pure, giving its due proportion, and no more, to the sympathetic, the human emotional element—a life, in all these, unhasting, unresting, untiring to the end" (*PW* 1:230). Poe renders service not by embodying this figure but by offering "that entire contrast and contradiction which is next best to fully exemplifying it." In this way, Whitman manages to absorb and praise Poe without compromising his own beliefs about poetry and life.

Thus graciousness, though in varying degrees, pervades Whitman's consideration of these six writers in *Specimen Days*. He approves almost everything, even when one approval sometimes contradicts another. Whitman argues, for example, that quiet, soothing Longfellow is "the sort of bard and counteractant most needed . . . for the present age in America" (*PW* 1:285). And yet Carlyle, the direct antithesis of Longfellow, is also crucial: "His rude, rasping . . . contradictory tones—what ones are more wanted amid the supple, polish'd, money-worshipping, Jesus-and-Judas-equalizing, suffrage-sovereignty echoes of current America?" (*PW* 1:261). The two remarks share only Whitman's approving voice and the notion that writers must work to counteract the age. In *Specimen Days*, Whitman seems most interested in maintaining his own consistently genial tone.

In the final decades of his life Whitman witnessed the deaths of other important writers of his day: Bryant in 1878, Carlyle in 1881, and Emerson and Longfellow in 1882. From the time of his paralytic stroke in 1873, Whitman had to reckon with the prospect of his own end. His mortality and suffering moved him, I believe, to emphasize his role as the enduring commentator. He was no longer able to brag of his perfect health, as he had at thirty-six in "Song of Myself," but his longevity did allow him to assess his fellows, to summarize their achievements, and to suggest lightly that they initiated a tradition which found full expression in his own work.

To the very end, Whitman continually adjusted his image to secure his role in American literature. One late jotting clarifies both how the "Tribute" functions within *Specimen Days* and why the war sections dominate this autobiographical record:

> Walt Whitman's second wind.
>
> Although the phrase may not be thought a very refined one, there is no description that so thoroughly hits the mark as the foregoing one borrowed from the vocabulary of the prize ring.
>
> There is a certain poise of self-pride about the book that offends many.
>
> It is very certain not only that its pages could not have been written anywhere else except in America and at the present, but that the Secession War, or as he calls it the "Union War" is their latent father, and that the result of that war gives an undertone or background of triumph and prophecy to every page. [*NUPM* 2:851]

To say that *Leaves of Grass* was born out of the Civil War is to ignore the fact that Whitman's best poetry was written before a shot had been fired. Yet, loosely speaking, *Leaves* was a response to sectional strife: the work was a vast recognition of the need for national spiritual renewal; its optimism, Whitman's willed reversal of his own dashed political hopes; its insistence on unity, a desperate attempt to resist the country's disintegration. But in the quoted passage Whitman was thinking more directly of the war period itself and of his self-sacrificial work in the hospitals. He frequently suggested that the hospitals offered a key to the war and that the war was *the* defining experience of the nation. Thus, his implicit argument runs, poets who lacked close contact with

the war—including Bryant, Longfellow, Poe, and Emerson—
could hardly speak for America. Only Whitman could claim to be
the poet of modern American *experience.*

In the early part of his career, Whitman was critical of his
fellow poets because they had failed to give adequate voice to
America and democracy, to science and the common man. And in
"Democratic Vistas" he asserted that "what finally and only is to
make of our western world a nationality superior to any hitherto
known, and outtopping the past, must be vigorous, yet un-
suspected Literatures, perfect personalities and sociologies, original, transcendental, and expressing (what, in highest sense, are
not yet express'd at all,) democracy and the modern" (*PW* 2:364).
Whitman believed that his contemporaries all fell short when seen
from this "democratic and western point of view" (*PW* 2:515). By
the time of *Specimen Days,* however, with his career nearly over
and *Leaves of Grass* in its final form, he directed his energies not to
pointing out shortcomings in others but to bolstering the Whitman myth. Thus, in writing both the autobiographical *Specimen
Days* and part of R. M. Bucke's *Walt Whitman,* he was asking (and
trying to answer) a question he had wondered about all through
his career: how would he be remembered? As a commentator on
other poets, he struggles to reconcile conflicting ends: benevolent
acceptance against sharp-edged critical assessment. Whitman
was enacting the role he had only envisioned before, the role of
the poet who synthesizes and subsumes his fellows and hence
explains his age.

CHAPTER FIVE

Sexual Equality and Marital Ideology:
Whitman and the Novel

O n March 1, 1882, *Leaves of Grass* was officially classified as obscene literature. Ironically, just when Whitman had asserted his centrality to American literature in *Specimen Days*, just when he was poised to achieve a new degree of recognition through publication by the established house of James R. Osgood, the district attorney of Boston judged his verse to be immoral and the postmaster banned *Leaves* from the mails. Yet notoriety had its advantages: when Osgood refused to contest the matter in court, *Leaves* was reissued by Rees Welsh & Co. of Philadelphia and, predictably, sold briskly, at least for a brief period. Already famous for his sexual themes, Whitman now became an even more powerful symbol and inspiration for various writers chafing under the convention of reticence. Until the final decades of the nineteenth century, as Henry James noted, novelists had neglected "whole categories of manners, whole corpuscular classes and provinces." There had been, James perceived, an "immense omission" in English and American fiction, "a mistrust of any but the most guarded treatment of the great relation between men and women, the constant world-renewal."[1] At the turn of the century, however, Whitman's example enlarged the realm of possibility, as a variety of writers—including Hamlin Garland, Kate Chopin, and E. M. Forster—strove to overcome gentility.

Harold Bloom notes that "Whitman has been an inescapable influence not only for most significant poets after him . . . but also for the most gifted writers of narrative fiction. This influence transcends matters of form, and has everything to do with the Whitmanian split between the persona of the rough Walt and the ontological truth of the real me."[2] Whitman fashioned both public and private selves in order to present even the most intimate of experiences, to highlight what genteel culture had evaded, denied, or repressed. Whitman insisted that the gap between what was experienced and what was expressed should be closed, that art—if it was to be serious, honest, and complete—must deal with sex. The famous eleventh section of "Song of Myself" provides a fine example of Whitman gaining access to the hidden life of his culture, the life "aft the blinds of the window":

> Twenty-eight young men bathe by the shore,
> Twenty-eight young men and all so friendly;
> Twenty-eight years of womanly life and all so lonesome.
>
> She owns the fine house by the rise of the bank,
> She hides handsome and richly drest aft the blinds of the window.
>
> Which of the young men does she like the best?
> Ah the homeliest of them is beautiful to her.
>
> Where are you off to, lady? for I see you,
> You splash in the water there, yet stay stock still in your room.

Dancing and laughing along the beach came the twenty-
   ninth bather,
The rest did not see her, but she saw them and loved them.

The beards of the young men glisten'd with wet, it ran
   from their long hair,
Little streams pass'd all over their bodies.

An unseen hand also pass'd over their bodies,
It descended tremblingly from their temples and ribs.

The young men float on their backs, their white bellies
   bulge to the sun, they do not ask who seizes fast to
   them,
They do not know who puffs and declines with pendant
   and bending arch,

They do not think whom they souse with spray.

[*CRE*, pp. 38–39]

For the nineteenth century, this voyeuristic passage was startling:
it depicts an independent woman (she "owns the fine house"),
acknowledges her sexual yearnings, describes these longings as
occurring outside of marriage, accepts nonprocreative sexuality,
and suggests that the "lady" crosses boundaries of age and class
consciousness in her fantasized life with carefree "young men"
rather than a dignified gentleman. Although Whitman was not
always consistent in his statements about female sexuality, it was
unconventional ideas such as these that most influenced novelists.

Shortly after the Boston suppression controversy, Whitman
recorded an important insight, arguing in "A Memorandum at a
Venture" (June 1882) that the prevailing conventional treatment
of sex in literature was the "main formidable obstacle" blocking
the "movement for the eligibility and entrance of women amid

new spheres of business, politics, and the suffrage" (*PW* 2:494).
Several recent critics have come to the same conclusion, contend-
ing that the emancipation of women required a greater candor
about sexuality.[3] Until the 1890s, marriage was rarely scrutinized
in fiction. Instead, writers focused on courtship: it offered sus-
pense and a clearly understood reward, it seemed to possess inherent form, and it dealt more with sexual attraction than with
sexual relationships. "Nothing so well marks [the modern] period," according to Carolyn G. Heilburn, as the "refusal to take
marriage for granted or to be content only to hint at its defects."
And the shortcomings of marriage could be surveyed only once
people had begun to speak candidly about sex and to understand
what marriage ought to have in common with friendship.[4] In the
closing decades of the nineteenth century, in both England and
America, people debated the virtues and failings of the institution
of marriage, especially the role of marriage in promoting polarized
gender roles and the submission of wives to husbands. Such writers as Garland, Chopin, and Forster, dissatisfied both with the
prevailing marital ideology and with the restricted scope of the
novel, gained inspiration from Whitman's candor, his self-con-
scious primitivism, his free love themes, his questioning of gender roles, his democratizing of relationships, and his focus on
companionship.

Unfortunately, twentieth-century critics frequently over-
simplify Whitman's ideas about women: too often the poet's
praise of motherhood is stressed to the exclusion of all else.
Granted: motherhood was important to Whitman's thought, and
the reproductive power of women is sometimes presented in
ways that modern readers find intrinsically limiting. Yet Whitman
also was able to envisage women with possibilities beyond "divine maternity," and it was his potentially liberating ideas that
influenced Hamlin Garland's *Rose of Dutcher's Coolly* (1895), Kate

Chopin's *The Awakening* (1899), and E. M. Forster's *A Room With A View* (1908). Garland, Chopin, and Forster offer important accounts of women's sexuality and depict heroines who yearn to be more than subservient beings. All three authors employ Whitman's ideal of comradeship as a means to highlight the limitations of conventional marriage. Whereas Garland and Forster endorse Whitman's ideals, Chopin, in her more pessimistic novel, both admires and laments them—admiring their attractiveness and lamenting their near impossibility for a nineteenth-century woman to realize. Chopin faces more squarely than either Garland or Forster the biological factor—the likelihood that sexual awakening might lead to pregnancy—and thus she accounts better for the painful conflict between liberation and reproduction.

Garland's Rose on the Open Road

Hamlin Garland created in *Rose of Dutcher's Coolly* one of the first American novels to depict the developing sexuality of a young girl as she matures into a woman—in this case, into a "new woman" of the 1890s intent on self-development and on establishing a love relationship based on equality rather than hierarchy. Of the many influences on *Rose*, Whitman may have been the most important.[5] Garland had admired Whitman since the mid 1880s, and by the early 1890s, when he began *Rose of Dutcher's Coolly*, he was ready to explore Whitman's theme of "healthy" sex in a full-length novel.[6]

Both the frank treatment of sexuality and the praise of "comrades" in *Rose* owe much to Whitman. Rose's sexuality is an issue throughout the book. In the opening pages, John Dutcher, a Wisconsin farmer, worries about rearing his daughter alone after the death of his wife. An inquisitive child, Rose asks her father how she came to be born. Dutcher feels awkward at even the thought of discussing reproduction with his daughter. Although he lacks intellectual sophistication and conversational skills, Dutcher is the first of four kind and sensitive older men in Rose's life. Father and daughter develop a relationship that will later serve as a model for other alliances: "her comradeship was sweet to John Dutcher" and he found himself "completely . . . companioned by Rose."[7]

In general, Garland is at pains to create in Rose a character free from prescribed gender roles. As a child, she chases gophers and bugs and beetles, leads her schoolmates in building a stove, excels in sports, and thinks nothing of having dirt and warts on her hands. Her "heart rebelled" the few times she encountered "sex distinction," once in winter, when the boys established the right to segregate the room so that they could set nearer the fire, and again in summer, when the boys drove the girls away from the swimming hole. Like Whitman's twenty-ninth bather, "she looked longingly at the naked little savages running about and splashing in the water. There was something so fine and joyous in it." It seemed unfair that the boys could "strip and have a good time, but girls must primp around and try to keep nice and clean."[8]

As if to underscore Rose's freedom from prescribed societal norms, Garland entitles the second chapter "Child-Life, Pagan Free." A type of pastoralism contributes to the depiction of Rose's sexuality. Garland's pastoralism is "less a matter of shepherdesses and sheep than a mode by which the civilized imagination exempts itself from the claims of its own culture."[9] Garland evades many of his culture's assumptions about women by lifting Rose out of time. Occasionally, when Rose was alone, "she slipped off her clothes and ran amid the tall corn-stalks like a wild thing. . . . Some secret, strange delight, drawn from ancestral sources, bubbled over from her pounding heart, and she ran until wearied and sore with the rasping corn leaves, then she sadly put on civilized dress once more." Again, after picking berries one June day, Rose and her friends become "carried out of themselves" as they respond to the "sweet and wild and primeval scene." They play games "centuries old" and enact mock marriage ceremonies. Rose, paired with Carl, has "forgotten home and kindred" as she lives "a strange new-old life, old as history, wild and free once more." When Carl puts his head in Rose's lap, she feels her first surge of passion and yearns "to take his head in her arms and kiss it. Her muscles ached and quivered with something she could not fathom."[10] Garland attempts to gain perspective by placing sex in a primal context, by moving "beyond culture" and the particular mores of time and place.[11] This, of course, was what Garland's contemporaries had seen Whitman accomplish. (Willa Cather wrote in 1896 that Whitman is "sensual . . . in the frank fashion of the old barbarians"; John Burroughs wrote in the same year that "Whitman has the virtues of the primal and savage"; and George Santayana argued in 1900 that Whitman possesses "the innocent style of Adam.")[12] Following Whitman, Garland employed what would become a central strategy of modernism: the revitalizing and reassessing of the present by means of the primitive.

Garland is inconsistent in his treatment of sex, however: sometimes he presents it in the light of primitive purity, but at other times he displays ambivalence about sex and the changing role of women. Garland waxes Whitmanian in his praise of "the healthy, wholesome physical." For example, Garland describes Rose's "fine and pure physical joy" when, in the secrecy of her room, "she walked up and down, feeling the splendid action of her nude limbs." Yet after arguing that the "sweet and terrible attraction of men and women towards each other is as natural and as moral as the law of gravity," Garland goes on to say: "Its perversion produces trouble. Love must be good and fine and according to nature, else why did it give such joy and beauty?" To Garland's way of thinking, Rose does not always act in harmony with "nature" for she experiences an "out-break of premature passion." Rose's experience, before the age of fifteen, of youthful petting with Carl is something she must "live down." The daring introduction of this theme is offset by Garland's brief, vague, and decorous treatment of it. Rose generally controls her passion because of her "organic magnificent inheritance of moral purity." The descendant of "generations of virtuous wives and mothers, [she is] saved . . . from the whirlpool of passion."[13] The quoted passages indicate that, despite Garland's attempt to move "beyond culture" and despite his ostensible acceptance of sexuality and freedom, he remained partly bound by conventional notions of purity and restraint.[14]

Rose moves beyond her physical attraction to Carl when she encounters William de Lisle, one of the circus performers, in the chapter entitled "Her First Ideal." Sexuality and spirituality, the real and the ideal, are not antithetical: these performers have "invested their nakedness with something which exalted them." Rose formulates her first "vast ambitions" when she dreams of being his "companion." William de Lisle does her "immeasurable good" because he moves her to yearn for comparable greatness as a scholar or writer and because he enables her to escape "mere brute passion" and an early marriage.[15]

It may seem incongruous that Garland links lofty aspirations to what is largely an erotic response. Yet for Garland the real and the ideal were not to be separated but united. Genteel writers failed, he believed, because they habitually divided life into exclusive spheres: love, art, and the ideal were opposed to sex and everyday experience. Garland, regarding himself as a "follower" of Whitman, attempted to break down restricting divisions. As he remarked in "The Evolution of American Thought," "the *idealization of the real* . . .underlies the whole theory of Whitman. . . . He is master of the real, nothing daunts him. The mud and slush in the street, the gray and desolate sky, the blackened walls, the rotting timbers of the wharf—the greedy, the ragged, the prostitute—vulgarity, deformity, all—no matter how apparently low and common, his soul receives and transforms."[16] Garland was committed to illustrating that Rose's sexual knowledge, experience, and fantasies produced neither personal nor social catastrophe. Instead, sex contributed to her overall development. No genuine understanding of Rose is possible, Garland implicitly argues, unless one perceives the difficulties and mistakes, the joy and general "healthiness" of her sexual life.

William de Lisle stands alone as Rose's ideal until she encounters Dr. Thatcher. While she attends the University of Wisconsin, Rose lives with the Thatcher family, and Dr. Thatcher becomes an ideal more "substantial" though "less sweet and mythical" than de Lisle. William de Lisle was a vision in the distance; Thatcher, as a married man, is also distanced from Rose, but at least she can regard him as an "uncle and adviser." Though Thatcher struggles with his more than avuncular attraction to Rose, he treats her with concern for her well-being, her intellectual development, and her growth as a person. William de Lisle had (unknowingly) helped her avert an early marriage by the power of his image; Thatcher tells Rose explicitly,"you will do whatever you dream of—*provided* you don't marry." Thanks to these men and Mrs. Spencer (a female role model who recommends marriage only after thirty), Rose leaves Madison alone and eager to embark on the "open road."[17]

Garland's reference to Whitman's "Song of the Open Road" is appropriate because the buoyant optimism of that poem matches the hopefulness of Garland's novel. (To reinforce this allusion, Garland entitles a later chapter "Rose Sets Face towards the Open Road.") Like Whitman, Rose has ordained herself "loos'd of limits and imaginary lines"; she goes where she chooses, her "own master total and absolute." When Rose moves to Chicago after college, she impresses nearly everyone with her talents. Only Warren Mason is critical. This brilliant, middle-aged newspaperman and frustrated novelist sees great potential in Rose, but he understands that her poetry thus far is derivative, that it does little more than echo English classics.

Through Mason, Garland expresses many of his own ideas. With regard to marriage, Mason has little faith in "sentiment and love-lore." Moreover, as he tells his friend Sanborn, he is troubled by the "possible woman." He "can't promise any woman to love her till death" because "another might come with a subtler glory, and a better fitting glamour, and then—." As Mason becomes increasingly attracted to Rose, he realizes that marriage might hinder her development. Eventually, by letter, Mason makes a proposal indebted to Whitman's ideals and language:

> I exact nothing from you. I do not require you to cook for me, nor keep house for me. You are mistress of yourself; to come and go as you please, without question and without accounting to me. You are at liberty to cease your association with me at any time, and consider yourself perfectly free to leave me whenever any other man comes with power to make you happier than I.
>
> I want you as comrade and lover, not as subject or servant, or unwilling wife. . . . You are a human soul like myself, and I shall expect you to be as free and sovereign as I, to follow any profession or to do any work which pleases you.[18]

In describing the Mason-Rose relationship, Garland draws on the spirit of "Song of the Open Road":

Camerado, I give you my hand!
I give you my love more precious than money,
I give you myself before preaching or law;
Will you give me yourself? will you come travel with me?
Shall we stick by each other as long as we live?

[*CRE,* p. 159]

The speaker in Whitman's poem offers the hope of permanency, whereas Mason promises only a limited loyalty. Nonetheless, Garland informs the reader that Mason's word "comrade" pleased Rose: "It seemed to be wholesome and sweet, and promised intellectual companionship never before possible to her."[19] The concept was far from pleasing to Garland's contemporaries, however, who, because of Mason's stress on personal freedom, feared that he was proposing a free love union or a trial marriage. Garland may indeed have had a marital experiment in mind, but he hastily retreated from any such suggestion when he revised the book in 1899 and ended it with an explicit mention of a civil wedding (never mentioned in the 1895 edition) and a glimpse of domestic bliss.[20]

In *Rose* Garland failed to integrate fully Whitman's themes with his own unconscious assumptions. The idea of comradeship is undermined because Garland too frequently depicts Rose as a follower. We are told that her father functioned as her "hero and guide," that William de Lisle was "a man fit to be her guide," that Dr. Thatcher's "dominion [over Rose] was absolute," and that Mason "always . . . dominated her."[21] Garland seems unaware that he has further weakened his praise of equality by presenting Rose as a character who really seeks another father rather than a comrade. The oedipal warp in her affections is unmistakable: de Lisle, Thatcher, and Mason are all significantly older than she is, and she regards men her own age as dull. Finally, Garland weakens his theme of equality by suggesting that Rose finds fulfillment and identity not in her self but in her union with Mason.

Some of the inconsistencies in *Rose* can be attributed to intellectual failings, but others probably resulted from Garland's own unresolved psychological conflicts. There is a strong autobiographical element in *Rose*, and—although Garland has reversed the sexual roles—one might speculate about the analogies between Rose's strong link to her father, movement to the city, development as a poet, and late marriage and Garland's own strong attachment to his mother, removal to Boston, growth as a writer, and long bachelorhood. Just as Rose's search for a comrade is undermined insofar as she sees men as heroes and guides, so too is Garland's use of Whitman—his literary father—damaging to the extent that he accepts Whitman's ideas uncritically and fails to make them his own. In many places the novel illustrates the accuracy of Henry James's harsh verdict on Garland: he was the "soaked sponge of his air and time."[22] Garland endorsed Whitman's ideas in *Rose*, but because he had not sufficiently internalized these ideas, the novel, for all its power, is at odds with itself.

Whitman's Twenty-Ninth Bather in Forster's Sacred Lake

In his use of Whitman's themes, E. M. Forster resembles Garland, though his treatment of these themes is more subtle. Forster drew inspiration from Whitman's poetry to promote a greater acceptance of sexuality and employed Whitman's idea of comradeship as a model for relationships between men and women. It is important to stress that at least by 1907, and probably earlier, Forster thought Whitman to be homosexual, as one of his diary notes indicates.[23] Some critics have argued that *A Room with a View,* published in 1908, is a crypto-homosexual novel embedded within what appears to be a traditional domestic comedy. What is certainly clear is that Forster had difficulty, throughout his career, in producing believable accounts of heterosexual love and that the single most convincing depiction of passion in this novel occurs during a homoerotic bathing scene reminiscent of section eleven of "Song of Myself."[24] Intriguingly, Forster transferred the values he associated with this scene and his insight into these personal relations to his treatment of the love between Lucy Honeychurch and George Emerson, the one fulfilling heterosexual relationship in Forster's fiction.

Whitman's impact on *A Room* has not been sufficiently acknowledged because critics have not appreciated how Forster manipulated names. Forster, as it were, reversed literary history by having his two characters named Emerson express Whitman's values and vision.[25] This transference of Whitman's ideas onto Mr. Emerson and his son George Emerson gave Forster certain advantages: the underpinnings of the novel appear to rest on the values of "a saint who understood" (Mr. Emerson), a saint related in name to the irreproachable sage of Concord. Yet George Emerson takes part in the crucial bathing scene that calls Whitman to mind, and both Mr. Emerson and George share Whitman's faith in sex and use Whitman's language. That Forster's Mr. Emerson and George are closer to Whitman than to Ralph Waldo Emerson is everywhere suggested: like Whitman, Mr. Emerson has been a journalist and is associated with socialistic causes; the Emersons are of the lower class; these Emersons frequently advocate "comradeship"; and the Emersons are convinced of the "holiness of direct desire." In a fine ironic touch, Forster has Mr. Emerson argue that we shall not return to the Garden until we cease to be ashamed of our bodies. Perhaps Forster knew that Ralph Waldo

Emerson had feared how the public would respond to Whitman's own return to the Garden in "Children of Adam."

To understand Forster's thinking about Whitman is to grasp a central theme of *A Room*—the contrast between a "medieval" and a modern vision. One year before the publication of *A Room*, Forster read a paper on Dante to the Working Men's College Literary Society, arguing there that

> Man consists of body and soul. So the middle ages thought, and so we think today. . . . We believe that a material element and a spiritual element go to make us up. . . . But—and here comes the difference—the middle ages thought that between the body and the soul one can draw a distinct line, that it is possible to say which of our actions is material, which spiritual. . . .
>
> Now I need hardly point out to you how different our attitude is today. He is a rash man who would assert where the body ends and where the soul begins. . . . Most modern thinkers realize that the barrier eludes definition. . . . It is there, but it is impalpable; and the wisest of our age, Goethe, for example, and Walt Whitman, have not attempted to find it, but have essayed the more human task of harmonizing the realms that it divides.[26]

Forster, in *A Room*, calls for more of the sort of poetry Whitman wrote when he described the union of body and soul in section five of "Song of Myself." Forster's character Mr. Emerson speaks for the author himself when he says: "I only wish poets would say this, too: that love is of the body; not the body, but of the body. . . . Ah for a little directness to liberate the soul."[27]

Italian settings and American ideas serve Forster in *A Room* as his means to reach "beyond culture" in his critique of marriage. As he traces the progress of his heroine Lucy, Forster endorses conclusions similar to those of Garland, though Lucy is markedly different from Rose. In *Rose* we witness a gradual increase in the heroine's culture and sophistication; in *A Room* Lucy learns to discard her early notions about gender, relationships, and class. Both Forster and Garland, drawing on Whitman, argue for marriage between equals and indicate that equality can be achieved only once women are recognized as sexual beings.

Early in the novel, in that portion set in Italy, we learn about Lucy's authentic self when we see her at the piano. Here she enters "a more solid world." "Like every true performer," Lucy was "intoxicated by the mere feel of the notes: they were fingers caressing her own; and by touch, not by sound alone, did she come to her desire." When Lucy sits at the piano she need no longer be "either deferential or patronizing; no longer either a rebel or a slave"[28]; like many other late-nineteenth-century heroines, she escapes the limits of her role through artistic sensibility. But her instinctual passionate force must fight against training and the social conventions that are enforced, in Italy, by Lucy's chaperone, Charlotte. Charlotte believes in the "medieval lady," though the dragons and knights are gone. Thus Charlotte informs Lucy that most "big things [are] unladylike." She explained that it is "not that ladies were inferior to men; it was that they were different. Their mission was to inspire others to achievement rather than to achieve themselves."[29]

Lucy engages in a quiet, unplanned revolt against the likes of Charlotte when she yearns to do something her well-wishers would disapprove of. Vaguely, hesitantly, Lucy intuits that the yearning she feels (and her sense of "muddle") results from repression of the body. At Santa Croce, she views Giotto's frescoes and hears two rival interpretations of the source of their power. The clergyman, Mr. Eager, contends that the paintings result from spiritual force; Mr. Emerson applauds their "tactile values." Throughout the novel Lucy is called on to balance and reconcile the (apparently) conflicting claims of the body and the soul. A few days after the scene at Santa Croce, Lucy has clearly begun to recognize the claims of the body: it is not accidental that she purchases photographs of "The Birth of Venus" and other nudes. While carrying her nudes, she witnesses a murder. When she falls into George Emerson's arms, love and death are emblematically united. Lucy has crossed a "spiritual boundary" as surely as the dead man. On the return home, George throws her pictures, now splattered with blood, into the river and—instead of "protecting" Lucy—tells her about the blood on them. She does not yet fully appreciate that he is treating her as an equal. But this idea is enforced by the first use of the key term "comrade." As Lucy and George lean together against the parapet of the embankment, the narrator comments: "There is at times a magic in identity of position; it is one of the things that have suggested . . . eternal comradeship." Lucy does not fully realize until much later that she was a "rebel . . . who desired . . . equality beside the man she loved." Italy was offering her "the most priceless of all possessions—her own soul," but she is slow to take it.[30]

One sees how faltering Lucy's progress is when she becomes engaged, shortly after her return to England, to a man who can imagine only one sort of relationship: a "feudal" one. Cecil Vyse thinks in narrow terms of "protector and protected"; he has no understanding of "the comradeship after which the girl's heart yearned." Part of George's appeal, in contrast, has always been that "in him Lucy can see the weakness of men." George accurately analyzes his rival when he remarks that Cecil "daren't let a woman decide. He's the type who's kept Europe back for a thousand years." When Lucy accuses George himself of similar behavior, he does not deny the charge but instead observes that the "desire to govern a woman—it lies very deep, and men and women must fight it together before they shall enter the Garden."[31]

The closest any of Forster's characters come to the Garden—to uniting body and soul, to reconciling animality and spirituality—occurs during the naked bathing scene in the Sacred Lake, a small pond near Windy Corner, where the Honeychurch family lives. Shortly after the Emersons move to Windy Corner, Lucy's brother Freddy suggests to George and Reverend Beebe that they "go for a bathe." As the upper-class Freddy, the lower-class George, and the clergyman strip, they shed restricting social distinctions and ennui. "It had been a call to the blood and to the relaxed will, a passing benediction whose influence did not pass, a holiness, a spell, a momentary chalice for youth."[32] When Cecil, walking through the woods with Lucy and her mother, encounters naked bodies and the clergyman's undergarments floating on the pond, he immediately tries to protect Lucy from this scene. As Bonnie Finkelstein points out, "the freedom of men to bathe naked, which Forster contrasts with the lack of freedom for women to do the same thing, points out [a] central theme of *A Room with a View*, the question of the freedom of women in society."[33] In the past, Lucy had bathed in the Sacred Lake until she was discovered by Charlotte.

In *Leaves of Grass* and *A Room with a View* (and, indeed, in *The Awakening*) outdoor bathing, along with more general references to the values associated with the "open air," represent an alternative approach to life, a life of spontaneity and freedom unbound by conventional indoor limitations. If, in its most extreme form, the Victorian ideal of woman was "the angel *in* the house," the woman outdoors, in immediate contact with nature, represents an anti-ideal which could free women from the restrictions of an artificial purity. It is clear that Lucy is beginning to move beyond indoor restrictions when she informs Cecil that she associates him with a room without a view. He knows enough to want to be associated with the open air. This key expression comes up again later in the novel: Lucy thinks she has overcome her inclinations toward George, but once in the "open air" she pauses, and (fortunately) follows her feelings rather than her socially conditioned thought.[34]

Lucy eventually marries George, a man better suited to her than Cecil. But since Forster has indicated that marriage—at the turn of the century—is generally oppressive and feudal, he makes it clear that she enters not the conventional institution, but rather the highest personal relation between two equal individuals, a relation based on "tenderness . . . comradeship, and . . . poetry"—that is, on "the things that really matter."[35] Appropriately, George and Lucy begin their married life in Italy, back in Mr. Emerson's old room, for they have both accepted his affirmative view of life. But Forster's ending is problematic. Like Garland, Forster offers a radical critique of marriage through much of his novel only to endorse the institution (admittedly revised through Whitman's concept of comradeship) by closing in the conventional way, with the union of the hero and heroine. Neither Forster nor Garland chose the open forms favored by Henry James in his later works. Forster, however, shared James's reservations about such endings, for he believed that it was false, in his time, to end a novel with a happy marriage.[36] Indeed, in an early draft of *A Room* he ends the novel by having George killed in a bicycle accident.[37] Forster rejected this ending, I believe, because he had invested so much personal hope in the novel, despite the distancing he achieved by transferring his own belief in homosexual comradeship onto his depiction of heterosexual love. As John Colmer notes, this transference produced a "creative tension between a personal ideology only belatedly raised to full consciousness and an alien social ideology enshrined in a literary form [domestic comedy] to which he was strongly attracted on stylistic grounds."[38] Marriage might frequently be corrupt, and heterosexual love hard for him to imagine, but for Forster's own well-being he had to believe in the value and possibility of personal relations based on comradeship.

The Awakening: *The Twenty-Ninth Bather at Sea*

When Kate Chopin wrote her fiction—usually in the family living room and "in the midst of much clatter"—she kept "at hand" copies of both Whitman's prose works and his *Leaves of Grass*.[39] Like Garland and Forster, Chopin was emboldened by Whitman's example. To Chopin, Whitman—almost alone among American writers—dealt frankly and freely with life. Other American writers, she believed, suffered in comparison to French writers because "limitations imposed on their art by their environment hamper a full and spontaneous expression."[40] Whitman's impact on *The Awakening* has been noted by many, including Lewis Leary, who describes the novel as "pervaded" with the spirit of "Song of Myself," and Elizabeth House, who finds numerous connections between the novel and "Out of the Cradle Endlessly Rocking." Chopin's biographer, Per Seyersted, goes so far as to label *The Awakening* Chopin's *Leaves of Grass*. Our understanding of this literary relationship can be clarified, however, once we perceive that Chopin did not passively accept the poet's ideas.[41] Instead, *The Awakening* offers a critique of Whitman's visionary ideas by testing them against the hard truths of experience—that is, against one nineteenth-century woman's social, psychological, and physiological circumstances.

Unlike Rose and Lucy, who move toward fulfillment in comradeship with Mason and George, Edna, when we first meet her in *The Awakening,* has already achieved wealth, social status, and marriage with the seemingly worthy Léonce Pontellier. (By shunning the form of the courtship novel, Chopin avoids even the implication that a woman achieves identity through marriage.) *The Awakening* is not "about sex," as some have argued, but is instead a record of Edna's desire to achieve identity after marriage, her struggle to become a full self. Chopin, like Forster, alludes to Whitman's scene with the twenty-nine bathers, though she puts the scene to different uses from the Englishman. We recall that section eleven of "Song of Myself" opens with an insistent repetition of the number twenty-eight. Chopin alludes to this scene through her own repetition of this number in a conversation early in the novel between the twenty-eight-year-old Edna Pontellier and her companion Robert Lebrun. Robert asks her,

> . . . "Didn't you know this was the twenty-eighth of August?"
> "The twenty-eighth of August?"
> "Yes. On the twenty eighth of August . . . a spirit that has haunted these shores for ages rises up from the Gulf. With its own penetrating vision the spirit seeks some one mortal worthy to hold him company, worthy of being exalted for a few hours into realms of the semi-celestials."[42]

Whereas Whitman presented a vignette of the woman "aft the blinds" in section eleven of "Song of Myself," Chopin goes much further, giving the full account of *her* twenty-ninth bather, providing a narrative of struggle, development, and death. Chopin uses Whitman in a tough-minded fashion, revising the poet in a number of ways. Whitman's unencumbered twenty-ninth bather "owned" her house on the hill; Edna Pontellier, in contrast, has a husband and children, and (much more typical for a nineteenth-century woman) owns very little. Her husband Léonce values the furnishings in his house because they are "his" and values Edna as his "possession."

Edna's development is sparked by encounters with contrasting people who nonetheless illuminate facets of Edna's own character. Two encounters are crucial to Edna's growth into an awareness of her own physical nature and her artistic potential: first, she experiences physical intimacy with the "mother woman" Adèle Ratignolle; second, she hears the music of the antisocial artist Mademoiselle Reisz. These experiences help Edna in her attempt to understand "her position in the universe as a human being, and to recognize her relations as an individual to the world within and about her." Like Whitman himself, Edna has always had a dual sense of self, aware of both "the outward existence which conforms" and "the inward life which questions." In her effort to close the gap between the two, Edna eventually will become even more radical than Whitman in her complete rejection of her conventional role. Early in the novel Edna has her first alluring invitation from the sea, promising an ultimate fusion of outer life and consciousness:

> The voice of the sea is seductive; never ceasing, whispering, clamoring, murmuring, inviting the soul to wander for a spell in abysses of solitude; to lose itself in mazes of inward contemplation.
>
> The voice of the sea speaks to the soul. The touch of the sea is sensuous, enfolding the body in its soft, close embrace.[43]

This experience is expressed in Whitmanian terms, as is clear from the abundance of participles, the imagery drawn from "Out of the Cradle," and the key phrase—"inviting the soul"—inspired by section five of "Song of Myself." Chopin has intertwined the

achieved by a guiding reliance on the past: "Not a whisper comes out of him of the old stock talk and rhyme of poetry. . . . No breath of Europe . . . seems ever to have fanned his face or been inhaled into his lungs." Whitman rejects the past but also demonstrates the impossibility of fully doing so. Though he yearns to be antiliterary and antitraditional, *his* followers (imagined right from the start) are not to be so revolutionary. Whitman announces "laws," sets "models," and creates a "new school."[1] The denier of tradition possessed the enabling ego of a tradition founder.

In the preceding chapters we have seen that Whitman fills more of a middle ground than the extreme images he crafted of himself suggest. He is more complicated, more varied, more flexible, and certainly more generally aware of multiple influences than has been realized. Both a great assimilator and a great transformer of literary tradition, he built his poetic practice on a careful balance of the old and the new. Aside from some anxiousness in his relationship with Emerson, Whitman is remarkably confident in his engagements with other writers. A number of factors contributed to his assurance: his broad responsiveness, which kept any single influence from seeming unduly threatening, his belief that English and American poets were both writing English poetry, and an awareness of his own gifts.

Before *Leaves of Grass*, many poets had called for American verse but had failed to break away decisively from English poetry. Because Whitman defined himself in opposition to the English poetic tradition (even while benefiting from it), he set a standard which has become the major alternative: most twentieth-century American poets follow the precedent of indigenous verse established by Whitman. For novelists—because of the difference in genre—he serves less directly as a guide, but he encourages treatment of neglected subject matter.

Still, Whitman presents a puzzle: why do even very intelligent figures, such as the Harvard poets, having recognized Whitman's importance, have such trouble making use of his undertaking? One reason is a fissure in American culture. A rift developed, beginning in the 1850s, widening to a chasm at the turn of the century, that produced "cultural bifurcation"—a sense that the American people and art were at odds. This ordering held that art required special training, refinement, and locales.[2] Whitman and his legacy clarify the difficulties and opportunities facing the American artist. The poet speaks to the need and dream to overcome such separations, to produce high art that will reach the people.

Whitman stands for revolt. His immediate intellectual successors understand this much, but they have difficulty channeling that sense of revolt, forgetting that he always sustained a very positive attachment to the culture he was revolting against. While *Leaves of Grass* is encompassing, the early-twentieth-century mind seems to be built instead on exclusiveness or a sense of partition. The early modernists, with their insistence upon divisions—Van Wyck Brooks's highbrow versus lowbrow, for example—create a sense of absolute divisions that obscures the true gift of Whitman. The poet is a synthesizer whose work eludes the paradigms of high and low, Brahmin and vulgarian, traditional and innovative. The early twentieth century misses his essential legacy when thinking in terms of either-or rather than both.

We sometimes forget that both texts *and* the individuals who write them become canonized. This is especially so in the case of autobiographical writers. The imaginative bond between devotee and writer exists only partly at the level of reading experience.[3] Later writers found assurance in the image of Whitman as founder: he was an author vilified then vindicated, mocked then admired. He managed to intertwine forces of literary prestige and antiliterary counter-culturalism by becoming himself a center of power while giving the impression that he stood outside all privileged positions. This has contributed to his importance for marginalized groups. Whitman has thus been compatible with innumerable later projects, projects of varying and sometimes even conflicting purposes. Such capaciousness is a mark of a truly vital tradition.

 NOTES

Prologue

1 Richard H. Brodhead, *The School of Hawthorne* (New York: Oxford University Press, 1986), p. ix.
2 See Lawrence Buell, "Introduction" to *Selected Poems: Henry Wadsworth Longfellow* (New York: Viking Penguin, 1988), p. viii.
3 Here and in the following paragraph I draw on Weisbuch, *Atlantic Double-Cross: American Literature and British Influence in the Age of Emerson* (Chicago: University of Chicago Press, 1986), p. xv.
4 Butler, "Against Tradition: The Case for a Particularized Historical Method," in *Historical Studies and Literary Criticism*, ed. Jerome J. McGann (Madison: University of Wisconsin Press, 1985), p. 39.
5 Butler, p. 39.
6 Brodhead, pp. 7–8.
7 Roy Harvey Pearce, *The Continuity of American Poetry* (Princeton: Princeton University Press, 1961), p. 57; Harold Bloom, *New York Review of Books* 26 (April 16, 1984), 6.

Chapter 1. Whitman's Persona and the English Heritage

1 Henry David Thoreau to Harrison Blake, 7 December 1856, in *The Correspondence of Henry David Thoreau*, ed. Walter Harding and Carl Bode (New York: New York University Press, 1958), p. 445.

2 Quoted in Justin Kaplan, *Walt Whitman: A Life* (New York: Simon & Schuster, 1980), p. 17.

3 Paul Zweig, *Walt Whitman: The Making of the Poet* (New York: Basic Books, 1984), p. 204.

4 On the importance of social class to Whitman's self-conception, see especially M. Wynn Thomas, *The Lunar Light of Whitman's Poetry* (Cambridge: Harvard University Press, 1987).

5 *The Journals of Bronson Alcott*, ed. Odell Shepard (Boston: Little, Brown, 1938), p. 290.

6 See Louisa's letter to Walt written on about November 6, 1867. Unless otherwise noted, all letters from Louisa to Walt can be located in the Trent Collection, Duke University, Durham, North Carolina. For permission to quote from unpublished letters and from marginalia, I would like to thank John L. Sharp III, Curator of Rare Books, Perkins Library, Duke University.

7 Louisa to Walt Whitman, October 2, 1863; December 17, 1868; June 6, 1871; June 13, 1871; April 19, 1873 (Hannah Heyde [Whitman] Collection, Library of Congress); and *WWWC* 4:514.

8 Whitman's annotations are on articles written between 1839 and 1857. However, since he may have purchased used copies of some of these magazines, it is often impossible to tell when he read a given article. Whitman's markings in different colored inks and his comments about his earlier markings do indicate, though, that he went over some of these items several times. Unless otherwise specified, all annotated clippings discussed in this study can be found in Duke's Trent Collection. Smaller collections of marginalia include those at Rutgers University, Middlebury College, the New York Public Library, and the Library of Congress.

9 Floyd Stovall, in *The Foreground of Leaves of Grass* (Charlottesville: University Press of Virginia, 1974), has recorded some of the annotations I discuss in this chapter. Though very useful, Stovall's treatment of the marginalia (chapters 8, 14, 15) is mainly a listing of Whitman's remarks. Stovall does not analyze the poet's struggle with the English tradition as a whole, nor does he compare Whitman's attitudes toward English literature with those of his fellow American poets.

10 See *Prose Writings of William Cullen Bryant*, ed. Parke Godwin (New York: D. Appelton, 1884), 1:31–32, and "Nationality in Literature," in *Literary Criticism of James Russell Lowell*, ed. Herbert F. Smith (Lincoln: University of Nebraska Press, 1969), p. 129.

11 "After a Lecture on Wordsworth," *The Poetical Works of Oliver Wendell Holmes* (Boston: Houghton Mifflin, 1975), p. 91; "American Literature," in *Whittier on Writers and Writing: The Uncollected Critical Writings of John Greenleaf Whittier*, ed. Edwin Harrison Cady and Harry Hayden Clark (n.p.: Syracuse University Press, 1950), p. 25; and *The Journals and Miscellaneous Notebooks of Ralph Waldo Emerson*, vol. 13, 1852–1855, ed. Ralph H. Orth and Alfred R. Ferguson (Cambridge: Harvard University Press, 1977), p. 84.

12 *LG 1855*, p. 5, and "An English and an American Poet," in *In Re Walt Whitman*, ed. Horace L. Traubel, Richard Maurice Bucke, and Thomas B. Harned (Philadelphia: David McKay, 1893), p. 27.

13 "Nationality in Literature," p. 122. For similar arguments regarding Shakespeare, see Bryant, "Shakespeare," *Prose Writings* 2:305, and Holmes, "Shakespeare," *Poetical Works*, p. 211. For Milton, see Lowell, "Nationality in Literature," p. 122.

14 "An English and an American Poet," p. 28. For Whitman on Milton, see *The Complete Writings of Walt Whitman*, ed. Richard Maurice Bucke, Thomas B. Harned, and Horace L. Traubel (New York: G. P. Putnam's Sons, 1902), 9:97–98.

15 See *Whittier on Writers*, pp. 33, 70; Emerson, *The Complete Works of Ralph Waldo Emerson* (Boston: Houghton Mifflin, 1903), 5:255–56; Emerson, *Journals and Miscellaneous Notebooks*, 4:312; 9:372, 376, 378; and *Literary Criticism of Edgar Allan Poe*, ed. Robert L. Hough (Lincoln: University of Nebraska Press, 1965), p. 75.

16 *Literary Criticism of Edgar Allan Poe*, p. 104.

17 "The Vanity and the Glory of Literature," *Edinburgh Review*, American Edition, 89 (1849), 159.

18 "Thoughts on Reading," *American Whig Review* 1(1845), 485. Also quoted in *The Complete Writings* 9:161.

19 "An English and an American Poet," pp. 27–28.

20 "R. M. Milnes' Life of Keats," *North British Review*, American Edition, 10 (1848), 41.

21 *NUPM* 1:222. Edward Grier notes that this passage was probably written in 1855 or 1856.

22 See William Wordsworth, "Lines Composed a Few Miles above Tintern Abbey," in *Poetical Works*, ed. Thomas Hutchinson (1904; rev. Ernest De Selincourt, Oxford: Oxford University Press, 1969), p. 164; and Samuel Taylor Coleridge, "On Poesy or Art," in *Criticism: The Major Texts*, ed. Walter Jackson Bate (New York: Harcourt Brace Jovanovich, 1952; rev. ed. 1970), p. 396.

23 *Walt Whitman's Workshop*, ed. Clifton Joseph Furness (Cambridge: Harvard University Press, 1928), p. 21. Whitman and the English poets did share some common ground on this issue. Wordsworth, for example, believed that poetry began with the corporeal eye. Only later did the English poet move away from the body.

24 "Modern Poetry and Poets," *Edinburgh Review*, American Edition, 90 (1849), 213.

25 In "Characteristics of Shelley," *American Whig Review* 5 (1847), 535, Whitman underlined, along with the quoted passage, this sentence: "His muse never treads the earth, except on her favorite stilts, egotism and agitation." In "Tennyson's Poems," *Blackwood's Edinburgh Magazine* 65 (1849), 455, Whitman underscored these lines: "It did not follow that he [Tennyson]

and his compeers always soared above us because they could no longer walk on a level with us. Men, in a dream, think they are flying when they are only falling." And in "Egotism. As Manifested in the Works and Lives of Great and Small Men," *Graham's Magazine* 27 (1845), 99, Whitman drew a line in the margin next to this passage: "The egotism of Wordsworth colors all his writings. He cannot go out of himself and sympathize with other grades and conditions of being, but 'he accommodates the shows of things to the desires of his mind,' and makes Nature and man talk in the Wordsworthian dialect."

26 "Christopher under Canvass," *Blackwood's Edinburgh Magazine* 65 (1849), 765.

27 *NUPM* 5:1778. Whitman oversimplifies here. Some British poets, especially the younger romantics, shared his displeasure at the political shifts of Wordsworth, Coleridge, and Southey. See, for example, Byron's "Dedication" to *Don Juan* and Shelley's "To Wordsworth" and "Peter Bell the Third."

28 Whitman doubted that Wordsworth's devotion to nature allowed for the necessary love for man. He commented on "To My Sister": "Wordsworth, it seems, is the originator of this kind of poem—followed here by Bryant, and others." Apparently he disliked the neglect of society implicit in Wordsworth's bidding his sister to devote her day to nature. He inserted a copy of "To My Sister," clipped from Charles Knight's *Half-Hours with the Best Authors*, in his copy of a review of "William Wordsworth," *American Whig Review*, n.s., 8 (1851), between 70 and 71. The article and the poem are in the Berg Collection of the New York Public Library. This article is also discussed in Roger Asselineau, "Whitman et Wordsworth," *Revue de Littérature Comparée* 29 (1955), 505–12.

29 The quoted phrase is from "Taylor's Eve of the Conquest," *Edinburgh Review*, American Edition, 89 (1849), 192. See also "Tennyson's Poems," p. 456.

30 "Taylor's Eve of the Conquest," p. 194.

31 See M. H. Abrams's discussion of the romantics' use of myth in *The Mirror and the Lamp* (London: Oxford University Press, 1953), p. 294.

32 *NUPM* 5:1770. This last judgment may seem surprising today, but we should recall that Keats's reputation was by no means high: in 1846 De-Quincey criticized Keats for trampling upon the English language "as with the hoofs of a buffalo" (see Aileen Ward, *John Keats: The Making of a Poet* [New York: Viking, 1963], p. 407). As noted above, Whitman read a review of Richard Monckton Milnes's *Life, Letters, and Literary Remains of John Keats* (1848), and it was only with the publication of this book that Keats's reputation began its gradual rise. See Douglas Bush, *John Keats: His Life and Writings* (New York: Macmillan, 1966), p. 206.

33 In "Characteristics of Shelley," p. 536, Whitman underlined these sentences: "We are wearied and bewildered with dancing up and down, when

we should take every step right onward. A metaphor or simile is only legitimately employed to make our course at once more rapid and more delightful."

34 "Taylor's Eve of the Conquest," p. 191. Above his own summarizing title, "truth of style," Whitman has written "a pure and masterly style." The poet has given the left column his full battery of scorings: underlinings, a line in the margin, and two pointing hands.

35 *NUPM* 5:1770.

36 *Language and Style in* Leaves of Grass (Baton Rouge: Louisiana State University Press, 1983), especially pp. 160, 170, 193, 199.

37 *Complete Writings* 9:33.

38 John F. Lynen, *The Design of the Present* (New Haven: Yale University Press, 1969), pp. 283, 289.

39 "Christopher under Canvass," p. 764.

40 In his poetry Whitman attempts to conceal the forward movement of literary time so that the present at any point will seem the same present. See Lynen, pp. 273–339, and Roy R. Male, "Whitman's Radical Utterance," *Emerson Society Quarterly* 60 (1970), 74.

41 "Taylor's Eve of the Conquest," p. 186. In the top margin Whitman wrote "Character" and drew a hand pointing to the left column.

42 See "The Prelude," *American Whig Review*, n.s., 7 (1851), 457; "Recollections of Poets Laureate. Wordsworth: Tennyson," *American Whig Review*, n.s., 9 (1852), 523; and *LG 1855*, p. 10. Whitman's interest in other poets was often as much biographical as it was critical. He frequently made note of the financial situation of English poets. See also *Complete Writings* 9: passim.

43 "R. M. Milnes' Life of Keats," p. 48. Whitman wrote in the top margin "Criticism" as his catchword describing the left column.

44 Note, for example, Whitman's comment in "Democratic Vistas": "Faith, very old, now scared away by science, must be restored, brought back by the same power that caused her departure—restored with new sway, deeper, wider, higher than ever" (*PW* 2:421).

45 "*Leaves of Grass:* A Volume of Poems Just Published," *Brooklyn Daily Times*, September 29, 1855; reprint, *In Re Walt Whitman*, p. 23.

46 "An English and an American Poet," p. 29.

47 Ibid., pp. 29–30.

48 "On Some of the Characteristics of Modern Poetry, and on the Lyrical Poems of Alfred Tennyson," *The Writings of Arthur Hallam*, ed. T. H. Vail Motter (New York: Modern Language Association, 1943), p. 184.

49 Note also the contrast between Hallam's idea about this "period of degradation" and Whitman's comment on the worth of the American present: "An age greater than the proudest of the past is swiftly slipping away, without one lyric voice to seize its greatness" ("An English and an American Poet," p. 28).

50 "An English and an American Poet," pp. 29–30.

51 Samuel Johnson in his "Preface to Shakespeare" writes that love is the universal agent on every stage but Shakespeare's. "For this probability is violated, life is misrepresented, and language is depraved. But love is only one of many passions; and as it has no great influence upon the sum of life, it has little operation in the dramas of a poet, who caught his ideas from the living world, and exhibited only what he saw before him" (*Criticism: The Major Texts*, p. 209). And Joseph Warton argued that "one of the most remarkable differences betwixt ancient and modern tragedy arises from the prevailing custom of describing only those distresses which are occasioned by the passion of love . . . which, by totally engrossing the theatre, hath contributed to degrade that noble school of virtue into an academy of effeminacy" (Walter Jackson Bate, *From Classic to Romantic* [Cambridge: Harvard University Press, 1946], p. 68).

52 In an undated manuscript note in the Trent Collection, Whitman wrote: "In the plentiful feast of romance presented to us, all the novels, all the poems really dish up one only figure—various forms and preparations of one only plot, namely, a sickly scrofulous crude amorousness. True, the malady described is the general one—which all have to go through, on their way to be eligible to Love, but this is not love." Also quoted in *NUPM* 4:1604.

53 Whitman disliked both "The Princess" and "Maud." A comment on a review suggests Whitman's reasons for disliking "Maud": "It is a love-story, rather tedious and affected, with some sweet passages" ("Tennyson's Poems," p. 461, and "Recollections of Poets Laureate," p. 523).

54 Exasperated at a reviewer's overly subtle account of the differences between poetry and prose, Whitman responded: "The best poetry is simply that which has the perfectest beauty—beauty to the ear, beauty to the brain beauty to the heart, beauty to the time & place[.] There cannot be a true poem unless it satisfies the various needs of beauty" ("Christopher under Canvass," p. 765).

55 See Coleridge, "On Poesy or Art," p. 395, and Hallam, "On Some of the Characteristics of Modern Poetry," p. 184.

56 "An English and an American Poet," pp. 31, 27.

57 Ibid., pp. 27–28.

58 See Morris Eaves, "Romantic Expressive Theory and Blake's Idea of the Audience," *PMLA* 95 (1980), 784–801.

59 See M. H. Abrams, p. 25; *Shelley's Prose: Or the Trumpet of a Prophecy*, ed. David Lee Clark (Albuquerque: University of New Mexico Press, 1954), p. 282; *The Letters of John Keats*, ed. Hyder Edward Rollins (Cambridge: Harvard University Press, 1958), 1:267; and John Stuart Mill, *Dissertations and Discussions* (1859; reprint, New York: Haskell House, 1973), 1:71.

60 I base my dating on Whitman's style—the fact that "Pictures" has seemed

to so many readers like a rudimentary version of *Leaves of Grass* —and on his treatment of other poets. By 1855 Whitman had decided to make no overt mention of predecessors. My dating is in disagreement with that offered by Edward Grier in *NUPM* 4:1295. Grier argues for an 1855 or later date based on inconclusive evidence concerning the type of paper Whitman used; he also asserts that Whitman's "curious line about Lascars sacrificing money to the sea seems to be related to the careful note he made of this fact, as if it were new to him in 'June 23d '57.'" We can be confident, however, that Whitman encountered this word well before 1857, for it appears in a poem he was familiar with, Longfellow's "The Building of the Ship" (1849).

61 "Tennyson's Poems," p. 461.

62 Ibid., p. 459.

63 *The Poems of Tennyson*, ed. Christopher Ricks (New York: Norton, 1972), p. 414. Whitman probably knew the 1842 version of the poem rather than its 1832 form. Ricks's edition gives a sense of the way "The Palace" changed through revision over the years.

64 Alastair W. Thomson, *The Poetry of Tennyson* (London: Routledge & Kegan Paul, 1986), p. 38.

65 See, for example, Christopher Ricks, *Tennyson* (New York: Macmillan, 1972), pp. 94–95, and W. David Shaw, *Tennyson's Style* (Ithaca, N.Y.: Cornell University Press, 1976), pp. 58–59.

66 Clyde de L. Ryals first pointed this out in *The Two Voices: A Tennyson Study* (Lincoln: University of Nebraska Press, 1964), p. 26.

67 See Gay Wilson Allen, *The Solitary Singer: A Critical Biography of Walt Whitman* (New York: New York University Press, 1955), p. 145.

68 For an illuminating study of the poems, see George H. Soule's "Walt Whitman's 'Pictures': An Alternative to Tennyson's 'Palace of Art,'" *ESQ* 22 (1976), 39–47.

69 *The Poems of Tennyson*, p. 414.

70 "'The Palace of Art' Revisited," *Victorian Poetry* 4 (1966), 157.

71 Soule, p. 42.

72 *The Poems of Tennyson*, p. 410. For Whitman's more favorable response to the French Revolution and its impact on *Leaves of Grass*, see Larry J. Reynolds, *European Revolutions and the American Literary Renaissance* (New Haven: Yale University Press, 1988), pp. 125–52.

73 Shaw, p. 58.

74 John Pettigrew, *Tennyson: The Early Poems* (London: Edward Arnold, 1970), p. 22.

75 For helpful recent discussions of this point, see M. Jimmie Killingsworth, *Whitman's Poetry of the Body* (Chapel Hill: University of North Carolina Press, 1989), chapters 2 and 5, and David Leverenz, *Manhood in the American Renaissance* (Ithaca, N.Y.: Cornell University Press, 1989), pp. 31–34.

Chapter 2. Whitman and Emerson Reconsidered

1 Shils, *Tradition* (Chicago: University of Chicago Press, 1981), p. 42.

2 See Winters, *In Defense of Reason* (New York: William Morrow, 1947), p. 587; Matthiessen, *The American Renaissance* (London: Oxford University Press, 1941), p. 522; Waggoner, *American Poets: From the Puritans to the Present* (Boston: Houghton Mifflin, 1968), p. 154; and Gelpi, *The Tenth Muse* (Cambridge: Harvard University Press, 1975), p. 157.

3 Loving, *Emerson, Whitman, and the American Muse* (Chapel Hill: University of North Carolina Press, 1982), pp. 195–96 n.

4 For Bloom's comment, see *Poetry and Repression: Revisionism from Blake to Stevens* (New Haven: Yale University Press, 1976), p. 260; Whitman's "master" remark is quoted in Justin Kaplan, *Walt Whitman: A Life* (New York: Simon & Schuster, 1980), p. 17.

5 See, for example, Clarence Gohdes, "Whitman and Emerson," *Sewanee Review* 37 (1929), 79–93.

6 *In Re Walt Whitman*, pp. 14, 15, and 24.

7 Ibid., p. 28.

8 John Townsend Trowbridge claimed that Whitman told him in 1860, "I was simmering, simmering, simmering; Emerson brought me to a boil." Loving correctly notes that there is something curious about Trowbridge's keeping this dramatic statement secret until 1902, ten years after the poet's death. See *Emerson, Whitman, and the American Muse*, p. 96.

9 Donald E. Pease, *Visionary Compacts: American Renaissance Writings in Cultural Context* (Madison: University of Wisconsin Press, 1987), p. 122. In 1871 Whitman was to yearn for a time when English literature would not "enslave us, as now, but, for our needs . . . breed a spirit like your own— perhaps, (dare we say it?) to dominate . . . even destroy what you yourselves have left!" (*PW* 2:407).

10 See Sean Wilentz, *Chants Democratic: New York City and the Rise of the American Working Class, 1788–1850* (New York: Oxford University Press, 1984), passim.

11 Clifton Joseph Furness, *Walt Whitman's Workshop: A Collection of Unpublished Manuscripts* (Cambridge: Harvard University Press, 1928), p. 73.

12 Emerson, *Journals and Miscellaneous Notebooks* 13:112.

13 Leverenz, "The Politics of Emerson's Man-Making Words," *PMLA* 101 (1986), 47.

14 *In Re Walt Whitman*, pp. 13–14.

15 Soule, "Walt Whitman's 'Pictures': An Alternative to Tennyson's 'Palace of Art,'" p. 40.

16 Emerson, *Journals and Miscellaneous Notebooks* 13:84; and *The Complete Works of Ralph Waldo Emerson*, Centenary Edition, ed. Edward Waldo Emerson (New York: Houghton Mifflin, 1903–1904), 5:36.

17 Duncan, "Changing Perspectives in Reading Whitman," in *The Artistic Legacy of Walt Whitman*, ed. Edwin Haviland Miller (New York: New York University Press, 1970), p. 96.

18 Lewis Hyde, *The Gift: Imagination and the Erotic Life of Property*, p. 169. In discussing Whitman's poems, I cite the earliest published version in book form, though I refer to works by their 1892 titles.

19 Duncan calls it "the spiritual testament of a self-realization" (p. 73).

20 *The Collected Works of Ralph Waldo Emerson*, ed. Robert E. Spiller and Alfred R. Ferguson (Cambridge: Harvard University Press, 1971), 1:10.

21 *The Collected Works of Ralph Waldo Emerson* 3:16.

22 Diane Wood Middlebrook, *Walt Whitman and Wallace Stevens* (Ithaca, N.Y.: Cornell University Press, 1974), pp. 44–45.

23 For a helpful discussion of these points, see John Gatta, Jr., "Whitman's Revision of Emersonian Ecstasy in 'Song of Myself,'" in *Walt Whitman: Here and Now*, ed. Joann P. Krieg (Westport, Conn.: Greenwood Press, 1985), pp. 173–83.

24 See Hyde, *The Gift*, pp. 160–215.

25 *The Collected Works of Ralph Waldo Emerson* 1:10.

26 Middlebrook, p. 75.

Chapter 3. The Artistry of *Leaves of Grass*

1 Quoted in V. K. Chari, "Whitman and the Language of the Romantics," *Études Anglaises* 30 (1977), 314.

2 See Hollis, "Reflections on Whitman's Moral Vocabulary," in *The Cast of Consciousness: Concepts of the Mind in British and American Romanticism*, ed. Beverly Taylor and Robert Bain (New York: Greenwood Press, 1987), p. 177.

3 Michael T. Gilmore, *American Romanticism and the Marketplace* (Chicago: University of Chicago Press, 1985), p. 4.

4 Brodhead, *The School of Hawthorne*, p. 19.

5 "An English and an American Poet," reprint, *In Re Walt Whitman*, ed. Horace L. Traubel et al. (Philadelphia: David McKay, 1893), p. 28.

6 John Olin Eidson, *Tennyson in America: His Reputation and Influence from 1827 to 1858* (Athens: University of Georgia Press, 1943), especially pp. 14, 22, and 23.

7 Here and throughout this paragraph I am indebted to Chari, "Whitman and the Language of the Romantics."

8 William Charvat, *The Profession of Authorship in America, 1800–1879*, ed. Matthew J. Bruccoli ([Columbus]: Ohio State University Press, 1968), p. 109.

9 Joseph Jay Rubin, *The Historic Whitman* (University Park: Pennsylvania State University Press, 1973), p. 62.

10 Rubin suggests that poems by Fitz-Greene Halleck and Nathaniel Parker Willis may also have influenced Whitman. See *The Historic Whitman*, pp. 46, 62.

11 *Law and Letters in American Culture* (Cambridge: Harvard University Press, 1984), p. 194.

12 C. Carroll Hollis, *Language and Style in* Leaves of Grass (Baton Rouge: Louisiana State University Press, 1983), p. 90.

13 Gay Wilson Allen "Introduction," *LG 1856*, pp. xiv–xv.

14 Alan Trachtenberg, "Whitman's Romance of the Body: A Note on 'This Compost,'" in *Medicine and Literature*, ed. Enid Rhodes Peschel (New York: Neale Watson, 1980), p. 189.

15 Allen, "Introduction," p. xx.

16 The phrase is Whitman's in "All about a Mocking-Bird," reprint, *A Child's Reminiscence*, ed. Thomas O. Mabbott and Rollo G. Silver (Seattle: University of Washington Book Store, 1930), p. 19.

17 In *Literary Friends and Acquaintances*, William Dean Howells asserted: "It is not too much to say that it was very nearly as well for one to be accepted by the *Press* as to be accepted by the *Atlantic*, and for the time there was no other literary comparison" (quoted in Portia Baker, "Walt Whitman's Relations with Some New York Magazines," *American Literature* 7 (1935), 275.

18 "All about a Mocking-Bird," p. 19.

19 Ibid., p. 20.

20 The musicality of Tennyson's famous "sweet and low" passage from the "Princess" is echoed in Whitman's lines beginning *"Blow! Blow!"*

21 See, for example, Vivian R. Pollak, "Death as Repression, Repression as Death: A Reading of Whitman's *Calamus* Poems," forthcoming in *The Mickle Street Review*.

22 Stephen E. Whicher, "Whitman's Awakening to Death: Toward a Biographical Reading of 'Out of the Cradle Endlessly Rocking,'" in *The Presence of Walt Whitman: Selected Papers from the English Institute* (New York: Columbia University Press, 1962), p. 22.

23 Leo Spitzer, *Essays on English and American Literature*, ed. Anna Hatcher (Princeton: Princeton University Press, 1962), p. 21.

24 Whitman's clipped copy of Shelley's "To the Skylark" is in the Trent Collection. His familiarity with the works by Wordsworth and Keats I assume on the basis of his known interest in romantic poets.

25 Whitman's phrase is quoted in Chari, p. 322.

26 Roger Asselineau, *The Evolution of Walt Whitman: The Creation of a Book* (Cambridge: Harvard University Press, 1962), 2:248.

27 Milton Hindus in "Whitman and Poe: A Note" is certain that Whitman "was consciously primitive" in his poetry and thus concludes that the many parallels he sees between "Out of the Cradle" and "The Raven" could not be "intentional" allusions (*Walt Whitman Newsletter* 3 [1957], 5–6). Ned J. Davison in "'The Raven' and 'Out of the Cradle Endlessly

Rocking'" is content to conclude that Whitman "derived artistic stimulation, consciously or not, from Poe" (*Poe Newsletter* 1 [1968], 6). A more intriguing interpretation, which argues for Whitman's purposeful use of Poe, is offered in Edwin Fussel's *Lucifer in Harness: American Meter, Metaphor, and Diction* (Princeton: Princeton University Press, 1973), pp. 128–34.

28 Davison, p. 5.

29 *I Sit and Look Out: Editorials from the Brooklyn Daily Times,* ed. Emory Holloway and Vernolian Schwarz (New York: Columbia University Press, 1932), p. 171.

30 Kelley C. Larson, *Whitman's Drama of Consensus* (Chicago: University of Chicago Press, 1988), p. 189.

31 I am indebted to my colleague Jeffrey N. Cox for several ideas in this paragraph.

32 *Critical Essays on Walt Whitman,* ed. James Woodress (Boston: G. K. Hall, 1983), p. 207.

33 Lewis Hyde, *The Gift: Imagination and the Erotic Life of Property* (New York: Random House, 1979), p. 179.

34 *The Poetical Works of Longfellow* (1893; reprint, Boston: Houghton Mifflin, 1975), p. 11. Longfellow used the title "L'Envoi" again much later in his career in *Ultima Thule* (p. 348).

Chapter 4. Crisis and Control in the Late Phase

1 Helpful discussions of the differences between Whitman's early and late poetry are found in Hollis, *Language and Style in* Leaves of Grass, especially chapters 2 and 3, and in M. Jimmie Killingsworth, *Whitman's Poetry of the Body* (Chapel Hill: University of North Carolina Press, 1989), chapters 4 and 5.

2 E. D. H. Johnson, *The Alien Vision of Victorian Poetry* (Hamden, Conn.: Archon, 1963), p. xvi.

3 The concept of the life review, borrowed from students of aging, has been applied effectively to Whitman by George Hutchinson in "Life Review and the Common World in Whitman's *Specimen Days,*" *South Atlantic Review* 52 (1987), 3–23.

4 Quoted in Alan Golding, "A History of American Poetry Anthologies," in *Canons,* ed. Robert Von Hallberg (Chicago: University of Chicago Press, 1984), p. 292.

5 *The Poetical Works of Longfellow,* p. 103, and Leaves of Grass: *A Textual Variorum of the Printed Poems,* ed. Sculley Bradley et al. (New York: New York University Press, 1980), 3:637.

6 Allen, *The Solitary Singer,* p. 443.

7 *Walt Whitman's Blue Book,* facsimile of the unique copy in the Oscar Lion Collection (New York: New York Public Library, 1968), 1:188.

8 David Cavitch, *My Soul and I: The Inner Life of Walt Whitman* (Boston: Beacon Press, 1985), p. 155.

9 Jerome Loving, *Walt Whitman's Champion: William Douglas O'Connor* (College Station: Texas A&M University Press, 1978), p. 76.

10 Quoted in Betsy Erkkila, *Whitman the Political Poet* (New York: Oxford University Press, 1989), p. 344.

11 Hollis, *Language and Style in* Leaves of Grass, p. 148.

12 Ralph W. Rader, "The Dramatic Monologue and Related Lyric Forms," *Critical Inquiry* 3 (1976), 140.

13 See Rader, p. 141, and *CRE*, p. 420.

14 Richard P. Adams, "Whitman's 'Lilacs' and the Tradition of Pastoral Elegy," *PMLA* 72 (1957), 479–87.

15 Helen Vendler, "Whitman's 'When Lilacs Last in the Dooryard Bloom'd' " in *Textual Analysis: Some Readers Reading*, ed. Mary Ann Caws (New York: Modern Language Association of America, 1986), pp. 132–43.

16 *Walt Whitman and the Civil War*, ed. Charles I. Glicksberg (1933; reprint, New York: A. S. Barnes, 1963), p. 175.

17 See Golding, pp. 291–92.

18 "Walt Whitman's Actual American Position," *West Jersey Press*, January 26, 1876; reprint, *Walt Whitman's Workshop*, pp. 245–46.

19 Because Whitman correctly described "Emerson's Books" as "ungracious," I have transformed his term to "graciousness" in describing his changed attitude toward other writers.

20 Jane Johnson, "Whitman's Changing Attitude toward Emerson," *PMLA* 73 (1958), 452.

21 See "Democratic Vistas" in *PW* 2:388–89.

22 Before being printed in *Specimen Days*, "My Tribute to Four Poets" appeared as part of a larger article in the May 7, 1881, issue of *The Critic* under the title "How I Get Around at Sixty and Take Notes." The "Tribute" began under the subtitle "I Call on Longfellow."

23 "Walt Whitman," *Scribner's Monthly* 21 (1880), 60, 62. Stedman revised this piece slightly for *Poets of America* (Boston: Houghton Mifflin, 1885). Stedman's criticisms truly bothered Whitman. In 1885 Whitman blamed the critic—in two different interviews—for originating the idea that he was unfriendly toward his fellow poets. See Herbert Bergman's "Whitman in June, 1885: Three Uncollected Interviews" in *American Notes & Queries*, o.s., 8 (1948), 52, 54.

24 The only important praise of another American poet that I can find in Whitman's published work between 1855 and the "Tribute" is in the famous open letter to Emerson of 1856 (and that letter, as I have argued, is filled with ambivalence). It should be observed that Whitman verbally praised American poets in an interview with the Philadelphia *Press*, March 3, 1880. See Herbert Bergman, "Whitman on His Poetry and Some Poets: Two Uncollected Interviews," *American Notes & Queries*, o.s., 8 (1950), 163–

64. But this interview was an exception. Gay Wilson Allen accurately sums up the poet's attitude toward other writers in 1872: "Whitman himself in his growing petulance with all opposition had become almost fanatical in this doctrine [that if he was right all other poets must be wrong], and it was so uncompromising a position—and one so automatically compromising to all other contemporary poets—that it must inevitably generate opposition on both sides. This doctrine would soon prey upon Whitman's mind and reputation like a fatal disease." See *The Solitary Singer*, p. 447.

In his role as a journalist Whitman was less critical of other writers. As the editor of the *Brooklyn Daily Times* in 1857 and 1858, he very briefly praised Emerson and James Russell Lowell and printed some poems of Longfellow. See *I Sit and Look Out: Editorials from the Brooklyn Daily Times*, ed. Emory Holloway and Vernolian Schwarz (New York: Columbia University Press, 1932), pp. 63–64, 214.

25 The quoted phrase comes from Whitman's own approving description of Carlyle (*PW* 1:250).

26 Beginning in 1880, Whitman frequently cited these four poets as having special value. He often switched his ranking of the four, but Emerson or Bryant always headed the list. See, besides the "Tribute," the interviews with the Philadelphia *Press*, March 3, 1880, and the Boston *Daily Globe*, August 24, 1881 (in Bergman's "Whitman on His Poetry and Some Poets," pp. 164–65); the interview with the Washington *Post*, June 28, 1885 (in Bergman's "Whitman in June, 1885," p. 54); and "Old Poets" in *PW* 2:659–60; and *WWWC* 1:56, 222; 2:518, 533; 3:190, 277. For a more negative assessment of these four poets, see Whitman's interview with the St. Louis *Post-Dispatch*, October 17, 1879 (in Robert R. Hubach's "Three Uncollected St. Louis Interviews of Walt Whitman," *American Literature* 14 [1942], 145).

27 Whitman may be referring to Emerson's poem "The Humble-Bee."

28 Emerson died on April 27, 1882. On May 6 Whitman paid his respects to him in *The Critic* with "By Emerson's Grave." This piece first appeared, then, almost exactly a year after the "Tribute." It is tempting but hazardous to use Whitman's statements here to explain the topmost ranking of Emerson in the "Tribute." Such an argument could be in danger of disregarding the shaping influence of death on Whitman's later opinion.

29 It should be noted that Whitman did not refer directly to Bryant in discussing poems on death in "Democratic Vistas." Nonetheless, Whitman could hardly have written the passage without having Bryant, considering his great popularity, in mind.

30 Later in his career Whitman became more explicit about Whittier's Puritanic Quakerism. In an interview with the Washington *Post* on June 28, 1885 (reproduced in Bergman's "Whitman in June, 1885," p. 54), Whittier is described as "especially fervid, rather grim, expressing a phase of Quaker Puritan element in New England history that is precious and rare beyond statement. I think in his old age he is inclined to be a little more

liberal and to get out of the narrow rut of Puritanic Quakerism." Similarly, in "Old Poets" Whitman says, "Whittier stands for morality (not in any all-accepting philosophic or Hegelian sense, but) filter'd through a Puritanical or Quaker filter. . . . Whittier's is rather a grand figure, but pretty lean and ascetic . . . not universal and composite enough" (*PW* 2:659–60).

31 See Whitman's own poem "As I Ponder'd in Silence" in *CRE*, pp. 1–2.

32 Whittier's poetry on the American Civil War refers repeatedly to Old World poets and heroes, such as Vaughan, Roland, Sidney, Shakespeare, and Cromwell. In formulating his statement on a Quaker war poet, Whitman probably had in mind his own war poetry and Quaker background. Of course *Drum-Taps* stands in marked contrast to Whittier's *In War Time.* Instead of "outcropping love of . . . war," verse in "measur'd step," and references to Old World figures, Whitman emphasizes his role as the wound-dresser, writes less regular verse, and celebrates the common soldier of the New World.

33 One can see Whitman gradually transforming Carlyle's political thought. In the 1871 essay "Democratic Vistas," Carlyle is the voice of feudalism. In the 1882 piece *Specimen Days,* Carlyle offers a protest against the fruits of feudalism. In a letter of 1886 to G. Oscar Gridley (*C* 6:34), Carlyle is thought "to be as much a democrat as anybody—more than a good many accepted ones." And, finally, on June 14, 1889, Carlyle is described as "a democrat of democrats—one of the truest that ever lived" (*WWWC* 5:291).

Chapter 5. Whitman and the Novel

1 *Theory of Fiction: Henry James,* ed. James E. Miller, Jr. (Lincoln: University of Nebraska Press, 1972), pp. 342–43.

2 *New York Review of Books* 26 (April 16, 1984), 6.

3 See, for example, Joseph Allen Boone, "Wedlock as Deadlock and Beyond: Closure and the Victorian Marriage Ideal," *Mosaic* 17 (1984), 65–81, and Annette Niemtzow, "Marriage and the New Woman in *The Portrait of a Lady,*" *American Literature* 47 (1975), 377–95.

4 "Marriage Perceived: English Literature, 1873–1941," in *What Manner of Woman: Essays on English and American Life,* ed. Marlene Springer (New York: New York University Press, 1977), pp. 168 and 171.

5 For an account of other influences on *Rose,* see Robert Bray, "Hamlin Garland's *Rose of Dutcher's Coolly,*" *Great Lakes Review* 3 (1976), 5.

6 Kenneth M. Price, "Hamlin Garland's 'The Evolution of American Thought': A Missing Link in the History of Whitman Criticism," *Walt Whitman Quarterly Review* 3 (1985), 1–20.

7 Garland, *Rose of Dutcher's Coolly,* ed. Donald Pizer (1895; reprint, Lincoln: University of Nebraska Press, 1969), p. 25.

8 Ibid., p. 17.

9 Linda Dowling, "The Decadent and the New Woman in the 1890's," *Nineteenth-Century Fiction* 33 (1979), 449.

10 *Rose*, pp. 19 and 29–31.

11 The quoted phrase is from Dowling, p. 450.

12 Cather's comment first appeared in the *Nebraska State Journal* for January 19, 1896; it is reprinted in *Critical Essays on Walt Whitman*, ed. James Woodress (Boston: G. K. Hall, 1983), p. 177. For Burroughs, see *Walt Whitman: The Critical Heritage*, ed. Milton Hindus (London: Routledge & Kegan Paul, 1971), p. 251. For Santayana, see "The Poetry of Barbarism," in *Interpretations of Poetry and Religion* (1900; reprint, New York: Harper & Row, 1957), p. 178.

13 *Rose*, pp. 310, 63, 128, 39, 83, 127, and 120.

14 Donald Pizer, "Introduction," *Rose*, p. xviii.

15 *Rose*, pp. 55, 61, and 62.

16 Price, "Hamlin Garland's 'The Evolution of American Thought,'" p. 14.

17 *Rose*, pp. 151 and 143.

18 Ibid., pp. 309, 380.

19 Ibid., pp. 382–83.

20 For differing interpretations of what kind of marriage Garland had in mind in the 1895 version, compare Pizer "Introduction," pp. xxxii–xxxiii, and Bray, "Hamlin Garland's *Rose of Dutcher's Coolly*," p. 14n11.

21 *Rose*, pp. 24, 60, 113, and 303.

22 The remark by James is quoted in B. R. McElderry, Jr., "Hamlin Garland and Henry James," *American Literature* 23 (1952), 435.

23 P. N. Furbank, *E. M. Forster: A Life* (London: Secker and Warburg, 1977), 1:159n, cites two lists. Robert Martin, "Edward Carpenter and the Double Structure of *Maurice*," *Journal of Homosexuality* 8 (1983), 35–46, first noted that the second list is made up of artists Forster believed to be homosexual.

24 Samuel Hynes comments on Forster's habit of writing crypto-homosexual stories: "one feels in so many of Forster's novels a kind of transference at work, as though one were reading a different sort of story, but translated into socially acceptable terms" (*Edwardian Occasions: Essays on English Writing in the Early Twentieth Century* [New York: Oxford University Press, 1972], p. 116). In "'Vacant Heart and Hand and Eye': The Homosexual Theme in *A Room with a View*," Jeffrey Meyers argues that "a fundamental questioning of the value of heterosexual love is recurrent in Forster's works" (*English Literature in Transition* 13 [1970], 185).

25 For a brief but helpful account of the influence of American transcendentalism on *A Room with a View*, see Herbert Howarth, "Whitman and the English Writers" in *Papers on Walt Whitman*, ed. Lester F. Zimmerman and Winston Weathers (Tulsa: University of Tulsa, 1970), p. 9. Howarth discusses effectively the presence of Emerson, Thoreau, and Whitman in *A Room with a View*, but he does not note the irony involved in Forster's giving to his character Mr. Emerson traits of Whitman.

26 Forster, *Albergo Empedocle and Other Writings,* ed. George H. Thomson (New York: Liveright, 1971), pp. 154–55.

27 Forster, *A Room with a View,* ed. Oliver Stallybrass (London: Edward Arnold, 1977), p. 202.

28 Ibid., pp. 29–30.

29 Ibid., p. 39.

30 Ibid., pp. 44 and 110.

31 Ibid., pp. 154 and 166.

32 Ibid., p. 133.

33 Bonnie Blumenthal Finkelstein, *Forster's Women: Eternal Differences* (New York: Columbia University Press, 1975), p. 67.

34 *A Room,* pp. 106 and 168.

35 Ibid., p. 202.

36 Forster, "Pessimism in Literature" (1906), in *Albergo Empedocle and Other Writings,* pp. 129–45.

37 Oliver Stallybrass, "Editor's Introduction," *A Room,* p. xvii.

38 John Colmer, "Marriage and Personal Relations in Forster's Fiction," in *E. M. Forster: Centenary Revaluations,* ed. Judith Scherer Herz and Robert K. Martin (Toronto: University of Toronto Press, 1982), p. 113.

39 See Kate Chopin's letter to Waitman Barbe, October 2, 1894, and [Sue V. Moore?,] "Mrs. Kate Chopin," *St. Louis Life* 10 (June 9, 1894), 11–12. Both items are reproduced in *A Kate Chopin Miscellany,* ed. Per Seyersted and Emily Toth (Oslo and Natchitoches: Universitetsforlaget and Northwestern State University Press, 1979), pp. 120 and 114–15.

40 William Schuyler, "Kate Chopin," *The Writer* 7 (August 1894), 115–17; reprinted in *A Kate Chopin Miscellany,* pp. 115–19.

41 See Lewis Leary, "Introduction" to Kate Chopin, *The Awakening and Other Stories* (New York: Holt, Rinehart, and Winston, 1970), p. xiii; Elizabeth House, "*The Awakening:* Kate Chopin's 'Endlessly Rocking' Cycle," *Ball State University Forum* 20 (1979), 53–58; and Per Seyersted, *Kate Chopin: A Critical Biography* (Baton Rouge: Louisiana State University Press, 1969), p. 162. My own thinking about the Chopin-Whitman relationship is perhaps closest to that of Otis Wheeler, who remarks that *The Awakening* involves "a rejection of the pervasive nineteenth-century faith in the individual, in spite of the Whitmanesque imagery. For what we see in Edna's story is a reversal of the Romantic dream of the unlimited outward expansion of the self" ("The Five Awakenings of Edna Pontellier," *The Southern Review* 11 [1975], 118–28). I would differ slightly from Wheeler, however, by arguing that Chopin does not so much reject this ideal as she laments the impossibility of realizing it.

42 *The Awakening,* in *The Complete Works of Kate Chopin,* ed. Per Seyersted (Baton Rouge: Louisiana State University Press, 1969), 2:909–10.

43 Ibid., 2:893.

44 Ibid., 2:893.

45 Ibid., 2:935 and 995.
46 Ibid., 2:896–97.
47 Hollis, *Language and Style in* Leaves of Grass (Baton Rouge: Louisiana State University Press, 1983), p. 134.
48 *The Complete Works of Kate Chopin* 1:202–03.
49 *The Awakening* 2:915 and 919.
50 See Anne Goodwyn Jones, *Tomorrow Is Another Day: The Woman Writer in the South, 1859–1936* (Baton Rouge: Louisiana State University Press, 1981), pp. 157–61, for a helpful discussion of sexual roles in the novel.
51 *The Awakening* 2:908.
52 Paula A. Treichler, "The Construction of Ambiguity in *The Awakening:* A Linguistic Analysis," in *Women and Language in Literature and Society*, ed. Sally McConnell-Ginet et al. (New York: Praeger, 1980), p. 244.
53 *The Awakening* 2:996.
54 Jones, p. 182.
55 Roy Harvey Pearce, *The Continuity of American Poetry* (Princeton: Princeton University Press, 1961), p. 254.

Chapter 6. Imagining Whitman at Harvard

1 Frank Lentricchia, "On the Ideologies of Poetic Modernism, 1890–1913: The Example of William James," in *Reconstructing American Literary History*, Harvard English Studies 13, ed. Sacvan Bercovitch (Cambridge: Harvard University Press, 1986), p. 222.
2 *A History of Modern Poetry: From the 1890s to the High Modernist Mode* (Cambridge: Harvard University Press, 1976), p. 100.
3 The term "great enabler" is Richard Brodhead's in *The School of Hawthorne* (New York: Oxford University Press, 1986) p. 8.
4 Charles Eliot Norton's perceptive review of the 1855 *Leaves of Grass* merits note as an example of Harvard's early interest in, if not complete approbation of, Whitman (*Putnam's Monthly* 6 [September 1855], 321–23).
    Joseph Trumbull Stickney, normally included in discussions of the Harvard poets, had little to say about Whitman; hence, I have omitted him from consideration. Perhaps because of the group Stickney seems closest to postmodernism, his reputation has been gradually rising, while that of the other Harvard poets, particularly Moody, has been falling. One might argue that Stickney is the exception that proves the rule concerning Whitman's importance to modernism—that is, in his postmodern tendencies, he bypassed Whitman altogether.
5 My thinking about male homosocial attachment in this period has been shaped by John W. Crowley, letter to Kenneth M. Price, February 3, 1988, and by Crowley's "Howells, Stoddard, and Male Homosocial Attachment in Victorian America," in *The Making of Masculinities*, ed. Harry Brod (Boston: Allen & Unwin 1987), pp. 301–24.

6 One example of Whitman's sometimes embittered attitude toward New Englanders is his "Of Emerson (& the New England Set)," a jotting that Whitman never published. See William White, "Whitman on New England Writers: An Uncollected Fragment," *New England Quarterly* 27 (1954), 395–96.

7 Alan C. Golding notes that around 1900 the "power to direct taste" began to shift from individual editors to an institution—the university. See "A History of American Poetry Anthologies," in *Canons*, ed. Robert Von Hallberg (Chicago: University of Chicago Press, 1984), p. 295.

8 Harold W. Blodgett, "Walt Whitman's Dartmouth Visit," *Dartmouth Alumni Magazine* 25 (February 1933), 13–15.

9 Brodhead, p. 56.

10 Ibid., p. 8.

11 Arnold T. Schwab, *James Gibbons Huneker: Critic of the Seven Arts* (Stanford: Stanford University Press, 1963), p. 81.

12 See Allen Walker Read, "The Membership in Proposed American Academies," *American Literature* 7 (May 1935), 155–57.

13 Quoted in Gay Wilson Allen, *Walt Whitman as Man, Poet, and Legend* (Carbondale: Southern Illinois University Press, 1961), p. 102.

14 See Golding, pp. 279–307.

15 "The Poetry of Barbarism," in *Selected Critical Writings of George Santayana*, ed. Norman Henfrey (Cambridge: Cambridge University Press, 1968), p. 91.

16 William James, "The Present Dilemma in Philosophy," in *Pragmatism and The Meaning of Truth* (Cambridge: Harvard University Press, 1978), p. 13.

17 "Walt Whitman: A Dialogue," in *Santayana on America: Essays, Notes, and Letters on American Life, Literature, and Philosophy*, ed. Richard Colton Lyon (New York: Harcourt Brace, 1968), p. 287.

18 Ibid., p. 288.

19 *The Sense of Beauty: Being the Outlines of Aesthetic Theory* (New York: Charles Scribner's Sons, 1896), p. 112.

20 *The Letters of George Santayana*, ed. Daniel Cory (New York: Scribner's, 1955), p. 62.

21 "Introduction" to George Santayana, *Interpretations of Poetry and Religion* (Cambridge: MIT Press, forthcoming).

22 "The Poetry of Barbarism," pp. 93–94.

23 Ibid., p. 95.

24 Ibid., p. 85.

25 See Mark Cumming, "Carlyle, Whitman, and the Disimprisonment of Epic," *Victorian Studies* 29 (Winter 1986), 221.

26 "Two Versions of the Genteel Tradition: Santayana and Brooks," *New England Quarterly* 55 (1982), 381.

27 "The Genteel Tradition in American Philosophy," *Winds of Doctrine* (New York: Scribner's, 1913), pp. 186–88.

28 Ibid., p. 192.

29 Ibid., p. 203.

30 Ibid., p. 193.

31 Henry Cabot Lodge apparently resisted Theodore Roosevelt's contention that his son's poems combined the characteristics of Marlowe and Whitman. See *Selections from the Correspondence of Theodore Roosevelt and Henry Cabot Lodge, 1884–1918* (New York: Scribner's 1925), 1:225.

32 In the spring of 1906, Lodge wrote to his friend Langdon Mitchell that "artistic perfection depends upon the degree to which the artist speaks his own words in his own voice and is unhampered by the vocabulary of convention and the megaphone of oratory—which exists and could exist only on the theory of an omnipresent multitude" (quoted in Henry Adams, *The Life of George Cabot Lodge* [1911; reprint, Delmar, New York: Scholars' Facsimilies, 1978], p. 190). Lodge hardly seems aware that his own work could be attacked on these very grounds.

33 *The Problem of Boston: Some Readings in Cultural History* (New York: W. W. Norton, 1966), p. 58.

34 John W. Crowley, "Whitman and the Harvard Poets: The Case of George Cabot Lodge," *Walt Whitman Review* 19 (1973), 165–66. For a broader discussion of Lodge as a Conservative Christian Anarchist, see Crowley, *George Cabot Lodge* (Boston: Twayne, 1976), pp. 50–67.

35 Crowley, *George Cabot Lodge*, p. 49.

36 Quoted by Crowley in "Whitman and the Harvard Poets," p. 167.

37 "Servae Laudes," quoted by permission of the Massachusetts Historical Society. Lodge's unpublished poems are gathered at the MHS in folders that have been dated (on the basis of handwriting and contextual information) by John W. Crowley.

38 The best discussion of the complicated development from "Servae Laudes" to "Whitman" is in an unpublished essay by Donna Hanna-Calvert, "George Cabot Lodge: His Poem to Whitman."

39 Stoddard's *South-Sea Idyls* (1873) is based in part on his amorous experiences with men on the Sandwich Islands and in Tahiti. He explained in a letter to Whitman of 1870 his motive in going to Tahiti: "I must get in among people who are not afraid of instincts and who scorn hypocrisy." Whitman "warmly" approved of Stoddard's "emotional and adhesive nature, & the outlet thereof." See Charley Shively, *Calamus Lovers: Walt Whitman's Working-Class Camerados* (San Francisco: Gay Sunshine Press, 1987), p. 138. For Stoddard's response to Lodge's poem entitled "Whitman," see the unpublished letter of November 10, 1900, Massachusetts Historical Society.

40 Unpublished typescript poem, quoted with permission of the Mas-

sachusetts Historical Society. Almost all of Lodge's unpublished poetry is in manuscript rather than typescript form. At one time Lodge may have intended to publish "Whitman," for the appearance of the typescript strongly suggests that it was meant to be printer's copy.

41 Crowley makes the same point. In one of his rare factual errors, however, he confuses "Whitman" and "Servae Laudes" (*George Cabot Lodge*, p. 61).

42 *Poems and Dramas of George Cabot Lodge* (Boston: Houghton, Mifflin, 1911), 1:122.

43 *The Life of George Cabot Lodge*, p. 150.

44 *Poems and Dramas of George Cabot Lodge* 1:117.

45 Maurice F. Brown, *Estranging Dawn: The Life and Works of William Vaughn Moody* (Carbondale: Southern Illinois University Press, 1973), p. 24.

46 Daniel Gregory Mason, "Introduction," *Some Letters of William Vaughn Moody* (1913; reprint, New York: AMS Press, 1969), p. vii, and Brown, p. 42.

47 Mason, "Introduction," p. xi.

48 *Some Letters of William Vaughn Moody*, p. 35.

49 Unpublished letter, n. d. Quoted with permission of Houghton Library, Harvard University.

50 See Brooks's poem "Misconceptions," apparently written in his freshman year at Harvard (1904–1905). The poem is printed in James Hoopes, *Van Wyck Brooks: In Search of American Culture* (Amherst: University of Massachusetts Press, 1977), p. 49.

51 See Brooks, *Scenes and Portraits: Memories of Childhood and Youth* (New York: Dutton, 1954), p. 106, and Douglas L. Wilson, "Introductory," in *The Genteel Tradition: Nine Essays by George Santayana* (Cambridge: Harvard University Press, 1967), pp. 19 and 20.

52 Brooks, *America's Coming-of-Age* (1915; reprint, New York: Octagon Books, 1975), p. 112.

53 Ibid., p. 133.

54 Edmund Wilson and Malcolm Cowley are quoted in Douglas L. Wilson, pp. 23–24.

55 See Howells's "Editor's Study," *Harper's* 83 (November 1891), 962–63; unpublished letter of November 10, 1900, from Stoddard to George Cabot Lodge, Massachusetts Historical Society; *The Selected Letters of William Carlos Williams*, ed. John C. Thirwall (New York: McDowell, Obolensky, 1957), p. 287; Stephen Tapscott, *American Beauty: William Carlos Williams and the Modernist Whitman* (New York: Columbia University Press, 1984), p. 66.

56 Masters's poem can be conveniently located in *Walt Whitman: The Measure of his Song*, ed. Jim Perlman, Ed Folsom, and Dan Campion (Minneapolis: Holy Cow! Press, 1981), p. 40.

57 Rolland, "America and the Arts," *The Seven Arts* 1 (November 1916), 50–51.

58 See Pound, "What I Feel About Walt Whitman," Markham, "Walt Whitman," and Rukeyser, "Whitman and the Problem of Good," in *Walt Whit-*

man: *The Measure of His Song*, pp. 31, 78, and 109. Theodore Roosevelt also compared Whitman to Dante in "Dante and the Bowery," *The Outlook* (August 26, 1911); reprint, Roosevelt, *Literary Essays* (New York: Scribner's, 1926), pp. 98–105.

Epilogue

1 *In Re Walt Whitman*, pp. 14–15.
2 Lawrence W. Levine, *Highbrow/Lowbrow: The Emergence of Cultural Hierarchy in America* (Cambridge: Harvard University Press, 1988), pp. 83–168.
3 See Lawrence Buell, "The Thoreauvian Pilgrimage: The Structure of an American Cult," *American Literature* 61 (1989), 199.

INDEX

Whitman, George Washington (brother), 13
Whitman, Louisa Van Velsor (mother), 12–13
Whitman, Thomas Jefferson ("Jeff"; brother), 11
Whitman, Walt: and the academy, 125; antiliterary claims of, 4, 34, 37–39, 56, 148–49; apprentice poems of, 57; and audience, 28, 53–56, 59, 61–62, 71, 73, 75; banned in Boston, 5, 96; on the body and creativity, 19; and the Civil War, 78, 94; and death, 67, 93; development of poetics, 14–28; and Egyptology, 30, 77; and Emerson, 3, 35–53, 79, 80, 82–85; family circumstances of, 11–12; as the "good gray poet," 73, 74, 75; and homosexuality, 44, 107, 123–24; influence on fiction, 6, 96–121; influence on world literature, 7; on love as poetic subject, 26–27, 158n52; metonymy, use of, 21–22; and myth, 21–22; and opera, 62; oppositional role of, 3, 6, 14, 34, 126; persona of, 8–9, 11; and primitivism, 24, 51; and Quakerism, 88, 89; rough pose of, 3, 24, 33, 53; self and poetic identity, 18–19; sexual themes of, 33–34, 44–45, 49–50, 96–100, 107, 114, 121; and slavery, 41–42, 160n9; and sympathy, 18–20; and time, 22; as tradition founder, 3, 6, 49, 149; and women, 98–100. Works: "albot Wilson" notebook, 9, 28; anonymous reviews of his own poetry, 24, 25, 26, 38, 61, 62, 148; "Birds of Passage," 72; "Calamus," 63, 123; "Children of Adam," 109; "Democratic Vistas," 87, 88, 95; "Emerson's Books (The Shadows of Them)," 79–80; "Excelsior," 72–73; "L'Envoy," 68–69; letter of 1856 to Emerson, 36–37, 39–45, 51, 52; "A Memorandum at a Venture," 98–100; "My Tribute to Four Poets," 80–88; "Out of the Cradle Endlessly Rocking," 56, 61–67, 78, 117, 119; "Passage to India," 138; "Pictures," 28–34, 37, 38, 45, 78, 158–59n60; "Pioneers! O Pioneers!," 73; "Prayer of Columbus," 74–75; Preface (1855), 10, 16, 20, 23, 26, 49; "Salut au Monde," 137, "So long!," 68–69; "Song of Myself," 45–52, 97–98, 115, 116–17; "Song of the Open Road," 104–06; Specimen Days, 71, 75, 80–88; "There Was a Child Went Forth," 78; "This Compost," 59–61; "Thou Mother with Thy Equal Brood," 71–72; "To Think of Time," 57–59, 78; "When Lilacs Last in the Dooryard Bloom'd," 71, 75, 77–79
Whitman, Walter, Sr. (father), 12, 38
"Whitman" (Lodge), 138–39
Whittier, John Greenleaf, 14, 15, 79, 126, 128; and Whitman, 80, 82–83, 87–88
Williams, William Carlos, 6, 124, 146
Wilson, Douglas L., 143
Wilson, Edmund, 145
Winters, Yvor, 36
Wordsworth, William, 28; and audience, 27; body and creativity, 19; and Whitman, 20, 23, 56, 64, 66
Wolfe, Thomas, 67

Young Sammy's First Wild Oats" (Santayana), 133

Zweig, Paul, 9